From Branson, With L.O.L.

Christopher James

Branson, Missouri, USA

Christopher James: From Branson with L.O.L.

Printed in the United States of America

ISBN: 978-0-615-63695-5

Learn more information at: funnyhypermagicboy.com

Dedicated to my wife Rachael, our twins, Alexander and Cassandra, and the one girl that can always make me laugh and smile, Olivia Vanessa

Contents

Book One:

The Jokes

There is never a shortage of material as a professional comedian. I find humor in every day life and situations, sometimes to the dismay of those around me. It's a gift and a curse. Over the years, I have found a career in comedy to not only be theraputic, but also very rewarding. People are never shy about sharing a joke or a funny annecdote after a show. One thing I have learned, everyone loves to laugh.

Anyone that has ever seen my show, knows that I like to have something for everyone. I include jokes for every age, lifestyle, and intellectual level. I like to include simple puns and annecdotes and few jokes that will make the audience think.

This book is a compilation of many things. First, it's jokes, stories and annecdotes I've collected over the years from audience members and friends. Second, it's my own style of humor and jokes from my show and personal life. Third, there are some jokes that I have purchased from professionals over the years. And last, it's some of the stories and jokes have been passed down over the years. Some oldies but goodies that still bring a smile, no matter how corny.

I've organized this book in the style of my own show. A mixture that will leave you thinking one minute, groaning the next, and laughing a paragraph later. Not every joke is for everyone. However, I feel there is something for everyone.

Enjoy.

A man dies and appears at the Pearly Gates. "Have you ever done a good deed?" asks St. Peter.

"Sure, one time I came across a gang of bikers who were threatening a woman," the man says. "I walked up to the leader and punched him the face, kicked over his bike, and told him, " You leave her alone, or you'll answer to me"

"That was very brave of you," says St. Peter. "When did this happen?"

"About five minutes ago."

A blonde who's having financial troubles decides to kidnap a child for ransom. She writes on a piece of paper: "I've kidnapped your son. Leave $10,000 behind the oak tree in the park tomorrow at 7 AM. The blonde." She walks over to the park, grabs a little boy, pins the note to his jacket and tells him to run home.

The next morning, the blonde goes back to the park, where she sees the boy standing behind the oak tree.

"I'm supposed to give you this," he says, handing her a brown bag. As she counts the money, she notices a new note pinned to his jacket: "For the records, I can't believe that one blonde would do this to another."

A man is feeling depressed and decides to see a psychiatrist. He gets to the office, lies down on the couch, and tells the doctor his life story.

"I know exactly what your problem is," says the psychiatrist. "It's a simple matter of low self-esteem."

"Oh," says the man, dejected.

"Don't worry," says the doctor. "It's very common among losers like you."

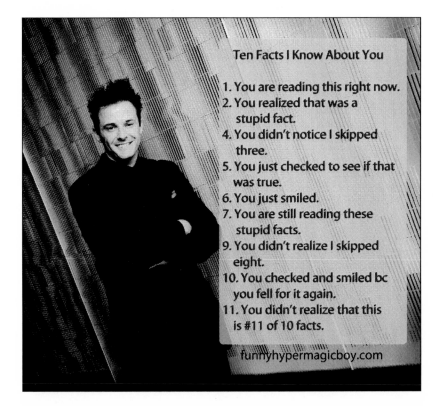

Ten Facts I Know About You

1. You are reading this right now.
2. You realized that was a stupid fact.
4. You didn't notice I skipped three.
5. You just checked to see if that was true.
6. You just smiled.
7. You are still reading these stupid facts.
9. You didn't realize I skipped eight.
10. You checked and smiled bc you fell for it again.
11. You didn't realize that this is #11 of 10 facts.

funnyhypermagicboy.com

An elderly man lying on his deathbed catches a whiff of homemade chocolate chip cookies wafting up the stairs. He gathers his strength and makes his way down to the kitchen. Just as he's reaching for the plate of cookies, his wife suddenly smacks him on the hand with a wooden spoon.

"Stay out of those," she yells. "They're for the funeral!"

On his first day at a new job, a guy attempts to phone an intern. "Bring me a cup of coffee pronto," he bellows.

"Do you know who you're talking to?" the voice on the other end of the line shouts back. "This is the president of the company!"

"Do you know who YOU are taking to, buddy?" the guy yells.

"No, I don't," replies the president.

"Thank goodness for that!"

My daughter and I have fun with Photoshop. We spent the summer making magic themed photos.

"I've found a great job," a man says to his wife. "A 10 AM start, a 6 PM finish, no overtime, no weekends, and it pays $2,000 a week in cash."

"That's unbelievable," says the wife.

"I know, "says the husband. "You start Monday."

A man approaches a beautiful woman in a supermarket.

"I've lost my girlfriend," he tells her. "Can you stand here and talk to me for a few minutes?"

"Sure, but I don't understand how that would help," she replies.

"Well, every time I talk to a beautiful woman like you, my girlfriend appears out of nowhere."

Doctors say I have a multiple personality, but we don't agree with that.

"I have some good news and I have some bad news," says the doctor.

"OK," says the patient. "Give me the good news first."

"Well," says the doctor, "they're going to name a disease after you..."

A redneck is walking down the road one day when he sees his cousin coming toward him carrying a gunnysack.

"Hey there, Billy Ray," says the redneck. "Whatcha got?"

"Some chickens," replies the cousin.

"If I kin guess how many you got, kin I have one?"

"Shoot, if you guess right, I'll give you both of 'em."

"OK...Five."

Little Amy is in her backyard filling a big hole with dirt, occasionally smacking it down with her shovel. Her curious neighbor peers over the fence. "What are you doing there, Amy?" he asks.

"I'm...I'm burying my goldfish, "she replies tearfully.

"Oh, sorry," he says, "but isn't that an awfully big hole for a goldfish?"

Amy pats down the last heap of earth, looks up, and says, "That's because he's inside your stupid cat!"

"I knew I had a problem with dyslexia the day I went to a toga party dressed as a goat"

A Frenchman with a parrot perched on his shoulder walks into a bar. The bartender says, "Wow, that's really neat! Where did you get him?"

"In France," the parrot replies. "They've got millions of 'em."

A burglar breaks into a house one night and turn on his flashlight to find an expensive stereo. As he approaches it, a voice behind him whispers, "Jesus is watching you."

The startled burglar turns and shines his light on a caged parrot in the corner of the room.

"Was that you?" asks the burglar.

"Yes," answers the parrot. "My name is Moses. How do you do? Squawk!"

Amused at the talking bird, the burglar laughingly asks, "What kind of people name a parrot Moses?"

"Squawk! The same kind of people who name a Rottweiler Jesus."

Dear Son:

I'm writing this slow cause I know you can't read fast.

We don't live where we did when you left. Your Dad read in the paper where most accidents happen within twenty miles of the house, so we moved. This place has a washing machine. The first day I put four shirts in it, pulled the chain, and haven't seen them since.

It's only rained twice this week. Three days the first time and four days the second time.

The coat you wanted me to send, your Aunt Sue said was too heavy to mail with all those big buttons on it so we cut them off and they're in the pockets.

We got a bill from the funeral home, said if we didn't make the last payment on Grandma's funeral, up she comes.

Your Uncle Joe fell in the whisky vat yesterday -- some men tried to pull him out but he fought 'em all off and finally drowned. We cremated him right after and he's still burning good this morning.

Three of your friends went off the bridge in a pick-up truck, one was driving, two in the back. The driver rolled the window down and swam out. The two in the back couldn't get the tailgate open so they drowned too.

Not much news this time, nothing much happens round here, will try to write more next time.

Love, Your Mama

P.S. Was gonna send you some money but already had this sealed up.

A blonde goes into the doctor's office and says that her body hurts wherever she touches it.

"That's odd, "says the doctor. "Show me what you mean."

The woman touches her elbow and screams in agony. She then touches her knee and screams, and then pushes on her ankle and screams.

"Just as I thought," says the doctor. "You have a broken finger"

"He who laughs last thinks slowest."

Q: Why did the blonde plant Cheerios in her garden?

A: She thought they were donut seeds.

Christopher's Photoshop is fun series:

"Today Dad and I hung around the house."

Two men are fishing on a riverbank when they see a funeral procession passing by. One of the men stands up, takes off his hat, and bows.

"That was a very nice thing to do," says the second man.

"Well," says the first, "we were married for 25 years."

"I've been told we only use 10% of our brains, imagine if we could learn to use the other 60%"

A redhead, a brunette, and a blonde are in a bar when the bartender tells them about a magic mirror in the ladies' room. Apparently, he says, the mirror gives rewards if you stare into it and say something true. But if you lie, you're sucked into the mirror and never heard from again.

So the redhead heads to the bathroom, looks into the mirror, and says, "I think I'm the most beautiful woman in this bar." A million dollars suddenly appears before her.

Then the brunette heads into the bathroom, looks into the mirror, and says, "I think I'm the smartest woman in this bar." The key to a new Ferrari materializes in her fingers.

Then the blonde goes in, looks into the mirror, and begins, "I think..." And she's sucked in and never heard from again.

A guy hears a knock at his door. When he answers it, there's nobody there, but there's a snail on the welcome mat. Frustrated, the guy picks up the snail and hurls it into the street.

Five years go by, and there's another knock at the door. The man answers it, and again there's no one standing there. But there's a snail on the welcome mat. The snail looks up and says, "What was that all about?"

Alcohol and calculus don't mix.

Never drink and derive.

I. Like. How. When. You. Read. This. The. Little. Voice. In. Your. Head. Takes. Pauses.

~Christopher James, 2011
The Wizard of Awed

wizardofawed.com
funnyhypermagicboy.com

Two guys decide to go bungee jumping in Mexico. Having never seen bungee jumping before, a crowd of locals gathers to watch. The first guy jumps and when he bounces back up, he's got cuts and bruises all over his face. The second guy helps him back onto the bridge. "What happened," he says. "Was the cord too long?"

"The cord was fine," he gasps, "It was the crowd. What's a piñata?"

My Grandmother once reflected that she wishes she could go back in time when...

-Decisions were made by going "eeny-meeny-miney-mo."

-Mistakes were corrected by simply exclaiming, "do over!"

-"Race issue" meant arguing about who ran the fastest.

- Money issues were handled by whoever was the banker in "Monopoly."

-Catching the fireflies could happily occupy an entire evening.

-It wasn't odd to have two or three "best friends."

-Being old referred to anyone over 20.

-The net on a tennis court was the perfect height to play volleyball and rules didn't matter.

-It was magic when dad would "remove" his thumb.

-It was unbelievable that dodge ball wasn't an Olympic event

-Having a weapon in school meant being caught with a slingshot.

-Scrapes and bruises were kissed and made better.

-It was a big deal to finally be tall enough to ride the "big people" rides at the amusement park.

-Getting a foot of snow was a dream come true.

-Abilities were discovered because of a "double-dog-dare."

-Saturday morning cartoons weren't 30-minute ads for action figures.

-"Oly-oly-oxen-free" made perfect sense.

-Spinning around, getting dizzy and falling down was cause for giggles.

-The worst embarrassment was being picked last for a team.

-War was a card game.

-Water balloons were the ultimate weapon.

-Baseball cards in the spokes transformed any bike into a motorcycle.

-Taking drugs meant orange-flavored chewable aspirin.

A wife sees a daytime talk show where they're discussing remarriage after a spouse passes away. After chatting with her mother and friends about it at length, she asks her husband later that night in bed, "Honey, if I were to die, would you remarry?"

He replies, "Well, after a considerable period of grieving and maybe even therapy...we all need companionship. So, I guess I would."

Spurred on by her husband's response, she then asks, "If I died and you remarried, would you let the woman live in this house?"

He replies, "We've spent a lot of money getting this house just the way we want it. It seems like a waste to give it all up...so, yes, I guess I would."

Looking flustered, the wife finally asks, "Would you let her use my golf clubs?"

"Oh no...she's left handed."

It's October, and an Indian chief thinks it's going to be a cold winter. So he instructs his tribe to collect wood.

To double-check his prediction, the chief calls the National Weather Service and asks a meteorologist if the winter is going to be a cold one.

25

The man responds, "According to our indicators, we think it might."

So the chief tells his people to find extra wood, just in case. A week later he calls the National Weather Service again, and they confirm that a harsh winter is headed their way.

The chief orders all his people to scavenge every scrap of wood they can. Two weeks later he calls the National Weather Service again and asks, "Are you absolutely sure this winter is going to be very cold?"

"Absolutely," the man replies. "The Indians are collecting wood like crazy."

This guy runs home and bursts in yelling, "Pack your bags, honey. I just won the lottery!"

She says, "Oh, wonderful! Should I pack for the beach or the mountains?"

He replies, "I don't care...just get out!"

"I can't stand it when people start something and don't fi

Christopher's Photoshop is fun series:

"Dad taught me how to hold my breath today."

A ventriloquist is touring clubs in Florida. With his dummy on his knee, he's going through his usual dumb blonde jokes when a blonde woman in the audience stands on her chair and shouts, "I've heard enough of your stupid blonde jokes. What does the color of a person's hair have to do with her worth as a human being? It's guys like you who keep women like me from being respected at work, and from reaching our full potential!"

The embarrassed ventriloquist starts to apologize, when the blonde yells, "You stay out of this, mister! I'm talking to that little guy sittin' on your knee!"

Be nice to your kids. They'll choose your nursing home.

A brother and sister are talking to each other when the little boy gets up and walks over to his grandfather. "Make a frog noise, Grandpa," he says.

"Why?" asks the grandfather.

"Please, please make a frog noise," pleads the boy.

"Not unless you tell me why."

"Because Mommy said when you croak we can all go to Disneyworld."

Always remember you're unique, just like everyone else.

*From my 2009 tour of Asia. Well, they tried.

Brian gets a parrot for his birthday. It has a bad attitude and a worse vocabulary. Every other word is offensive. Brian tries to change the bird's behavior with polite words, soft music...but nothing works. Out of desperation, he throws the bird in the freezer. It squawks, kicks, screams, and then falls silent. Brian, worried, swings the freezer door open. The parrot calmly steps out. "I believe I may have offended you with my rude language and actions. I will endeavor at once to correct my behavior."

Brian is amazed at the change in the bird's attitude and is about to ask what caused it when the parrot continues, "May I ask what the chicken did?"

A woman goes into a funeral home to make arrangements for her husband. She tells the director she'd like him to be buried in a dark blue suit.

"Wouldn't it be easier to bury him in the black suit he is wearing?" he asks. But she insists on dark blue and gives him a blank check to buy one with.

The woman returns for the wake later that day and sees her husband in the coffin wearing a dark blue suit.

"It's beautiful, " she says. "How much did it cost?"

"Nothing," says the director. "After you left, a corpse with a blue suit was brought in. They were about the same size so I asked his widow if she would mind if her husband was buried in a black suit. She said fine, so...I switched the heads."

A genii offers to grant a man one wish.

"Build me a bridge to Hawaii, " says the man, "so I can drive over anytime."

The genii says, "Think of the logistics of that kind of undertaking. The supports to reach to the bottom of the Pacific. The concrete and steel it would take. I can do this, of course, but it's hard for me to justify your desire for worldly things. Take a little time and think of another wish."

The man thinks for a while and says, "I wish I could understand women."

After a moment, the genii says, "You want two lanes or four?"

———————————————————————

A little man walks into a biker bar and clears his throat. "Um, which of you gentlemen owns the Doberman tied to the parking meter?"

A big biker turns slowly on his stool, "It's mine. Why?"

"Well," squeaks the little man, "I believe my dog just killed it."

"What?" bellows the biker in disbelief. "What kind of dog you got than can take down my Doberman?"

"Sir," answers the little man meekly, "it's a Chihuahua."

"A Chihuahua! A Chihuahua?" shouts the biker. "How could a little Chihuahua kill a Doberman?"

"Well, it appears that he choked on it, sir."

―――――――――――――――――――――――

Three guys die in a car crash and meet St. .

"When you're in your casket and your friends and family are gathered around, what would you like to hear them say?" St. Peter asks.

"I'd like to hear someone say I made a difference," answers the first guy.

"I'd like to hear someone say I was a good family man, " answers the second guy.

"And you?" St. Peter asks the third guy.

"I guess I'd like to hear someone say, 'Look! He's moving!'"

―――――――――――――――――――――――

Photoshop is fun series:

"Today Dad and I decided to cookout

Radio conversation released by the chief of naval operations 10.10.95...

Americans: Please divert your course 15 degrees to the north to avoid a collision.

Canadians: Recommend you divert YOUR course 15 degrees to the south to avoid a collision.

Americans: This is the captain of a US Navy ship. I say again, divert YOUR course.

Canadians: No, I say again divert YOUR course.

Americans: THIS IS THE AIRCRAFT CARRIER USS ENTERPRISE; WE ARE A LARGE WARSHIP OF THE US NAVY. DIVERT YOUR COURSE NOW.

Canadians: This is Rocky Point Lighthouse. Your call.

Farmer Joe is suing a trucking company over injuries he suffered in an auto accident. The company's layer begins to cross-examine the plaintiff.

"Isn't it true you said, 'I'm fine,' at the scene of the accident?" asks the lawyer.

"Well, I'll tell you what happened," farmer Joes starts.

"Did you or did you not say, 'I'm fine!'" thunders the lawyer.

"Let me explain," pleads the farmer. "I had just loaded my mule Daisy into the trailer and was driving down the highway when this semi-truck crashed into us. I was hurt real bad. When the highway patrolman came on the scene, he heard Daisy moaning and groaning. He took one look at her, pulled out his gun, and shot her between the eyes.

Then he came across the road with his gun in hand, looked at me, and said, "Your mule was in such bad shape I had to shoot her. How are you?"

"I've been thinking about this a lot lately, and I'm pretty sure my favorite Wookie is Chewbacca."

An elderly man in Miami calls his son, Dave, in New York and says, "I hate to ruin your day, but your mother and I are divorcing. Forty years of misery is enough! I'm sick of her, and I'm sick of talking about this so call your sister in Chicago and tell her," and then hangs up.

The son frantically calls his sister, who goes nuts upon hearing the news.

She calls her father and yells, "You are NOT getting a divorce! Dave and I will be there tomorrow. Until then, don't do a single thing, do you hear me?"

The father hangs up the phone, turns to his wife, and says, "It worked! The kids are coming for a visit, and they are paying their own way!"

A man walks into a bar, sits down and orders a drink. He says "Give me a drink before problems start!" The bartender doesn't understand but gives the man a drink.

After 15 minutes the man orders a drink again saying "Give me a drink before problems start!" The bartender looks a little bit confused but pours the man a drink.

This goes on the whole night and after the 15th drink the bartender is totally confused and asks the man "What do you mean with before problems start? And when are you going to pay for all the drinks you drunk."

The man answers "You see, now the problems start!"

Two friends get lost during a hiking trip through the desert. Several days later, they are dehydrated and near death.

Out of nowhere, they see a tree in the distance that appears to be covered with bacon. One guy sprints ahead, only to be gunned down in a hail of gunfire.

"Run!" the dying man yells out. "It's not a bacon tree. It's a ham bush!"

Q: How many psychiatrists does it take to change a light bulb?

A: One, but the bulb has got to want to change itself.

———————————————————————

A guy walks into the doctor's office with a banana stuck in one ear, a cucumber in the other and a strawberry wedged in his nostrils.

"Doc, I need help," says the guy. "Something's wrong with me."

"Well," says the doctor, "I can see you're not eating right."

———————————————————————

"I hate it when I accidentally use the same word too many times in a sentence accidentally."

———————————————————————

A man takes his Rottweiler to the veterinarian and says, "My dog is going cross-eyed. Is there anything you can do to help him?"

"Well," replies the vet, "let's have a look at him." So he picks up the dog and checks its eyes.

After a quick exam, the vet turns to the owner and says, "I'm afraid I'm going to have to put him down."

"Why? Just because he's cross-eyed?"

"No," says the vet, "It's just that he's really heavy!"

Actual Call Center Calls

Customer: "I've been calling 700-1000 for two days and can't get through; can you help?"
Operator: "Where did you get that number, sir?"
Customer: "It's on the door of your business."
Operator: "Sir, those are the hours that we're open."

Caller: "Can you give me the telephone number for Jack?"
Operator: "I'm sorry, sir, I don't understand who you are talking about."
Caller: "On page 1, section 5, of the user guide it clearly states that I need to unplug the fax machine from the AC wall socket and telephone Jack before cleaning. Now, can you give me the number for Jack?"

Operator: "I think it means the telephone plug on the wall."

Directory Enquiries
Caller: "I'd like the number of the Argo Fish Bar, please"
Operator: "I'm sorry, there's no listing. Are you sure that the spelling is correct?"
Caller: "Well, it used to be called the Bargo Fish Bar but the 'B' fell off."

Then there was the caller who asked for a knitwear company in Woven.
Operator: "Woven? Are you sure?"
Caller: "Yes. That's what it says on the label -- Woven in Scotland "

On another occasion, a man making heavy breathing sounds from a phone box told a worried operator: "I haven't got a pen, so I'm steaming up the window to write the number on."

Tech Support: "I need you to right-click on the Open Desktop."
Customer: "OK."
Tech Support: "Did you get a pop-up menu?"
Customer: "No."
Tech Support: "OK. Right-Click again. Do you see a pop-

up menu?"

Customer: "No."

Tech Support: "OK, sir. Can you tell me what you have done up until this point?"

Customer: "Sure. You told me to write 'click' and I wrote 'click'."

Tech Support: "OK. At the bottom left hand side of your screen, can you see the 'OK' button displayed?"

Customer: "Wow! How can you see my screen from there?"

Tech Support: "OK, the computer should be telling you to press any key."

Customer: ....

Tech Support: "Let me know when you are ready to move on."

Customer: "I keep looking and looking and I can't find the "any key"."

Tech Support: "Now, to install the program, we need to insert the CD."

Customer: "And where do I do that?"

Tech Support: "The CD drive in the front of your computer, push the eject button and the tray should open."

Customer: "CD player? I've been using that as a cup holder!"

Tech Support: "Press the left button on your computer mouse to continue."

Customer: "I'm trying but my toe won't reach."

Tech Support: "Your toe?"

Customer; "Yes, I thought you used the mouse like my sewing machine peddle, am I doing it wrong?"

A blonde walks into a library, goes up to the front desk, and says, "I'm here to see the doctor."

"This is a library, dearie," says the librarian.

"Oh, I'm sorry," whispers the blonde. "I'm here to see the doctor."

A married couple is walking past their neighbors' house. "Dave and Linda are so loving toward each other," says the wife. "Every time he sees her, he gives her a big kiss...unlike someone I know."

"Hey, I'd love to," says the husband. "But I don't know her that well."

Did you hear about the dyslexic agnostic insomniac?

He stayed awake all night wondering if there really was a dog.

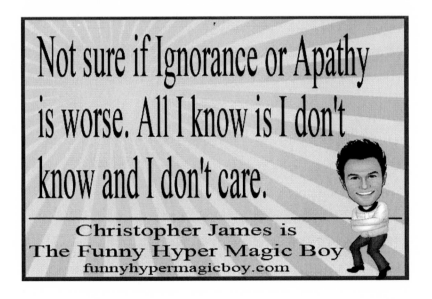

Not sure if Ignorance or Apathy is worse. All I know is I don't know and I don't care.

Christopher James is The Funny Hyper Magic Boy
funnyhypermagicboy.com

A man and a woman were having dinner in a fine restaurant. Their waitress, taking another order at a table a few paces away, noticed that the man was slowly sliding down his chair and under the table, with the woman acting unconcerned.

The waitress watched as the man slid all the way down his chair and out of sight under the table. Still, the woman dining across from him appeared calm and unruffled, apparently unaware that her dining companion had disappeared.

After the waitress finished taking the order, she came over to the table and said to the woman, "Pardon me, ma'am, but I think your husband just slid under the table."

The woman calmly looked up at her and replied firmly, "No he didn't. He just walked in the door."

ATTORNEY: She had three children, right?
WITNESS: Yes.
ATTORNEY: How many were boys?
WITNESS: None.
ATTORNEY: Were there any girls?

ATTORNEY: How was your first marriage terminated?
WITNESS: By death.
ATTORNEY: And by whose death was it terminated?

ATTORNEY: Can you describe the individual?
WITNESS: He was about medium height and had a beard.
ATTORNEY: Was this a male or a female?

ATTORNEY: Is your appearance here this morning pursuant to a deposition notice which I sent to your attorney?
WITNESS: No, this is how I dress when I go to work.

ATTORNEY: ALL your responses MUST be oral, OK? What school did you go to?
WITNESS: Oral.

A blonde is on a date with a geography teacher. "Believe it or not, I know all the state capitals," she says proudly.

"Oh, yeah?" says the guy. "What's the capital of Wisconsin?"

"That's easy," she replies. "It's a W."

Photoshop is fun series:

Olivia is shaping up to be an excellent babysitter.

A general is giving the president his daily briefing. He concludes by saying: "Yesterday, 3 Brazilian soldiers were killed in an accident'
"OH NO!" the President exclaims. "That's terrible!"

His staff sits stunned at this display of emotion, nervously watching as the President sits, head in hands. Finally he looks up and asks.......... "How many is a Brazillion??!'

"I hate it when people misspell obviuos words"

Sherlock Holmes and Dr. Watson go on a camping trip, set up their tent, and fall asleep. Some hours later, Holmes wakes his faithful friend.

"Watson, look up at the sky and tell me what you see."

Watson replies, "I see millions of stars."

"What does that tell you?"

Watson ponders for a minute. "Astronomically speaking, it tells me that there are millions of galaxies and potentially billions of planets. Astrologically, it tells me that Saturn is in Leo. Time wise, it appears to be approximately a quarter past three. Theologically, it's evident the Lord is all-powerful and we are small and insignificant. Meteorologically, it seems we will have a beautiful day tomorrow. What does it tell you?"

Holmes is silent for a moment, and then speaks. "Watson, you idiot, someone has stolen our tent."

Q: What do you call a musician without a girlfriend?

A: Homeless.

Q: Where's the English Channel?

A: I don't know - our television doesn't pick it up.

Life lessons from my Grandfather

1. Trouble in marriage often starts when a man gets so busy earnin' his salt that he forgets his sugar.

2. Too many couples marry for better, or for worse, but not for good.

3. When a man marries a woman, they become one; but the trouble starts when they try to decide which one.

4. If a man has enough horse sense to treat his wife like a thoroughbred, she will never turn into a nag.

5. On anniversaries, the wise husband always forgets the past - but never the present.

6. The bonds of matrimony are a good investment only when the interest is kept up.

7. Many girls like to marry a military man - he can cook, sew, and make beds and is in good health, and he's already used to taking orders.

8. Eventually you will reach a point when you stop lying about your age and start bragging about it.

9. The older we get, the fewer things seem worth waiting in line for.

10. Some people try to turn back their odometers. Not me, I want people to know "why" I look this way. I've traveled a long way and some of the roads weren't paved.

11. How old would you be if you didn't know how old you are?

12. I don't know how I got over the hill without getting to the top.

13. One things no one tells you about aging is that it is such a nice change from being young.

14. Ah, being young is beautiful, but being old is comfortable.

15. Old age is when former classmates are so gray and wrinkled and bald, they don't recognize you.

16. If you don't learn to laugh at trouble, you won't have anything to laugh at when you are old.

Two guys are in a bar.

First one: "My wife is an angel"

Second one: "You're lucky! Mine is still alive."

An English teacher wrote the words, "Woman without her man is nothing" on the blackboard and asked the students to punctuate it so that it made sense.

The boys wrote: "Woman, without her man, is nothing."

The girls wrote: "Woman! Without her, man is nothing."

Just before Thanksgiving Jim and Eddie are out hunting for turkeys when Jim keels over and collapses. He doesn't seem to be breathing and his eyes are glazed. Eddie gets out his cell phone and calls the emergency services.

He gasps, "My friend Jim is dead! What can I do?"

The operator says, "Calm down, I can help. First, let's make sure he's dead."

There's a silence, then a shot is heard.

Back on the phone, Eddie says, "OK, now what?"

A man follows a woman with a parrot out of a movie theater. He stops her and says, "I'm sorry to bother you, but I couldn't help but notice that your bird seemed to understand the movie. He cried at the right spots, he was fidgeting in his seat during the boring parts, and he laughed at the jokes. Don't you find that unusual?"

"I do indeed," she replies. "He hated the book."

One day a teacher was giving a lecture on philosophy, and had the class enthralled. It was a brilliant lecture.

Suddenly, over his head a bright light flashed and a genii papered and approached the teacher.

She said, "You are doing such a good job teaching this class, I have decided to give you one wish. You can have infinite money, infinite wisdom, or infinite knowledge."

Thinking for a minute, he humbly asked for infinite wisdom. She tapped him with a magic wand and disappeared in a flash. The class came forward to hear the first words from a man with infinite wisdom.

He said, "It would have been wiser to take the money..."

A man tells his doctor he's unable to do all the things around the house that he used to do. After the exam, he says, "Now, doc, I can take it. Tell me in plain English what is wrong with me."

"In layman's terms, you're lazy," says the doctor.

"Ok, now give me a medical term, so I can tell my wife."

Charles Dickens walks into a bar and orders a Martini.

The bartender says "Olive or Twist?"

Oh heavens, I do believe I have soiled my pantaloons...

My son is already shaping up to be quite the gentleman

-Christopher

A foolproof method for sculpting an elephant: get a huge block of marble, and then chip away everything that doesn't look like an elephant.

Grandma reflects on living in the 60s VS. being over 60

Then: Long hair.

Now: Longing for hair.

Then: Moving to California because it's cool.

Now: Moving to California because it's warm.

Then: Trying to look like Marlon Brando or Elizabeth Taylor.

Now: Trying not to look like Marlon Brando or Elizabeth Taylor.

Then: Getting out to a new, hip joint.

Now: Getting a new hip joint.

Then: Rolling Stones.

Now: Kidney stones.

Then: Peace sign.

Now: Mercedes logo.

Then: Passing the driver's test.

Now: Passing the vision test.

Then: "Whatever"

Now: "Depends"

A man returns from Africa feeling very ill. He visits his doctor, who immediately rushes the guy to the Mayo Clinic.

The man wakes up to the ringing of a telephone in a stark room at the hospital and answers it. "We've received the results from your tests," says the doctor on the other end of the line. "Bad news, you have Ebola."

"Oh, my," cries the man. "Doc! What am I going to do?""

"Don't' worry. First, we're going to put you on a diet of pizza, pancakes, and pita bread." Says the doctor.

"Will that cure me?"

"No, but it's the only food we'll be able to get under the door."

Bacon and Eggs walk into a bar...

The bartender says "Sorry, we don't serve breakfast."

A frog telephones the Psychic Hotline and is told, "You're going to meet a beautiful young girl who will want to know everything about you."

The frog says, "This is great! Will I meet her at a party or what?"

"No," says the psychic, "next term in her biology lesson."

A passenger train is creeping along, slowly. Finally it creaks to a halt. A passenger sees a conductor walking by outside. "What's going on?" she yells out the window. "Cow on the track!" replies the conductor.

Ten minutes later the train resumes its slow pace. Within five minutes, however, it stops again. The woman sees the same conductor walk again.

She leans out the window and yells, "What happened? Did we catch up with the cow again?"

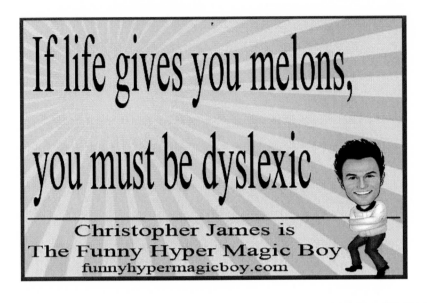

If life gives you melons, you must be dyslexic

Christopher James is The Funny Hyper Magic Boy
funnyhypermagicboy.com

An artist asked the gallery owner if there had been any interest in his paintings on display at that time.

"I have good news and bad news," the owner replied, "the good news is that a gentleman enquired about your work and wondered if it would appreciate in value after your death.

When I told him it would, he bought all 15 of your paintings."

"That's wonderful," the artist exclaimed, "what's the bad news?"

"The guy was your doctor..."

A businessman enters a tavern, sits down at the bar, and orders a double martini on the rocks.

After he finishes the drink, he peeks inside his shirt pocket, and orders another double martini. After he finishes that one, he peeks inside his shirt pocket again and orders yet another double martini.

The bartender says, "Look, buddy, I'll bring ya' martinis all night long - but you gotta tell me why you look inside your shirt pocket before you order a refill."

The customer replies, "I'm peeking at a photo of my wife. When she starts to look good, I know it's time to go home."

Two guys are talking while sitting on a bench in the park. "All of my ancestors followed the medical profession." said the first.

"Doctors?" queried the second.

"Nope. Undertakers and lawyers."

The new employee stood before the paper shredder looking confused.

"Need some help?" a secretary, walking by, asked.

"Yes," he replied, "how does this thing work?"

"Simple," she said, taking the fat report from his hand and feeding it into the shredder.

"Thanks, but where do the copies come out?"

Q: What is the difference between a Southern zoo and a Northern Zoo?

A: At Southern Zoos the animal descriptions include cooking times.

Humor in Church

Q. What kind of man was Boaz before he married Ruth?

A. Ruthless.

Q. What do they call pastors in Germany?

A. German Shepherds.

Q. Who was the greatest financier in the Bible?

A. Noah. He was floating his stock while everyone else was in liquidation.

Q. Who was the greatest female financier in the Bible?

A. Pharaoh's daughter. She went down to the bank of the Nile and drew out alittle prophet.

Q. What kind of motor vehicles are in the Bible?

A. Jehovah drove Adam and Eve out of the Garden in a Fury. David's Triumphwas heard throughout the land. Also, probably a Honda, because the apostleswere all in one Accord.

Q. *Who was the greatest comedian in the Bible?*

A. Samson. He brought the house down.

Q. What excuse did Adam give to his children as to why he no longer lived in Eden ?

A. Your mother ate us out of house and home.

Q. Which servant of God was the most flagrant lawbreaker in the Bible?

A. Moses. He broke all 10 commandments at once.

Q. Which area of Palestine was especially wealthy?

A. The area around Jordan. The banks were always overflowing.

Q. Who is the greatest babysitter mentioned in the Bible?

A. David. He rocked Goliath to a very deep sleep.

Q. Which Bible character had no parents?

A. Joshua, son of Nun.

Q. Why didn't they play cards on the Ark?

A. Because Noah was standing on the deck.

Did you know it's a sin for a woman to make coffee?Yup, it's in the Bible. It says. . 'He-brews'

There were two men in a building site. One of them said, "Can you help me find my ear?"

The other one, holding up an ear, asked, "Is this it"

"No" replied the first one, "mine has a pencil behind it"

Q: How many visitors to an art gallery does it take to change a light bulb?

A: Two. One to do it, and one to say "Huh! My four-year old could've done that!"

"If there are any idiots in the room, will they please stand up," said the sarcastic teacher. After a long silence, one freshman rose to his feet.

"Now then, mister, why do you consider yourself an idiot?" enquired the teacher with a sneer.

"Well, actually I don't," said the student, "but I hate to see you standing up there all by yourself."

Christopher Columbus was the best deal-maker in history. He left not knowing where he was going, and upon arriving, not knowing where he was. He returned not knowing where he had been, and did it all on borrowed money.

A worker was called to the office by his supervisor for talking back to his foreman.

Supervisor: "Is it true that you called him a liar?"

Worker: "Yes, I did."

Supervisor: "Did you call him stupid?"

Worker: "Yes."

Supervisor: "And did you call him an opinionated, bullheaded egomaniac?"

Worker: "No, but would you write that down so I can remember it?"

A bald man took a seat in a beauty shop. "How can I help you?" asked the stylist.

"I went for a hair transplant" the guy explained, "but I couldn't stand the pain. If you can make my hair look like yours without causing me any discomfort, I'll pay you $5000."

"No problem," said the stylist and she quickly shaved her head.

A man walks into a bar, sits down and says to the girl next to him, "Hey, you want to hear a great blonde joke?"

"Listen, buddy," the girl replies. "You can surely tell that I AM blonde. My three friends here are both world ranked judo masters and they're blonde too. Now, do you still want to tell that joke?"

"Nah," the man replies, "I don't feel like explaining it three times."

LOST GIRAFFE

"Franky"

Approx 15'4". Long Neck. Last seen near Branson Landing. Friendly. House Trained.

contact
funnyhypermagicboy.com

Olivia and I once spent spring break posting these all over town. You would be surprised at how many people emailed asking if this was serious.

Two cannibals are eating a clown. One says to the other, "Hey, does this taste funny to you?"

A cop pulls over a couple for speeding. He walks up to the driver and says, "I clocked you doing 80 mph, sir."

"Gee, officer," says the driver, "I had it on cruise control at 60."

"Don't be silly, dear," the wife chimes in. "This car doesn't have cruise control."

As the cop begins to write the ticket, the husband growls to his wife, "Can't you just keep your mouth shut?"

The wife smiles and says, "You should be happy the radar detector went off when it did."

"A radar detector, eh?" says the officer. "Those are illegal in this state." He starts to write up a second ticket.

"Will you please keep your mouth shut!" screams the husband to the wife.

The officer bends down, looks at the woman and asks, "Does he always talk to you like that?"

"Oh, heavens no," she replies, "Only when he's been drinking."

Two elderly couples are playing bridge, and at one point the wife go into the kitchen. One of the gentlemen says, "Last night we went to a really fantastic restaurant. I highly recommend it."

"What is the name of it?" the other man asks.

The first man thinks for a while and finally says, "Hey, what's the name of that flower? You know, it's red and has thorns on its stem."

"You mean a rose?"

"Yeah, that's it." He turns toward the kitchen and yells, "Rose, what's the name of that restaurant we went to last night?"

A man joins a Tibetan temple. He takes a vow of silence but is allowed to say two words every year.

After a long 12 months of eating rice, sleeping on a wooden bed with an old blanket, and working 14 hours a day in the fields, the man goes to the head monk and says, "More blankets."

Another year passes, and he visits the head monk and says, "More food."

The man goes through one more year eating good meals and sleeping well, but he's drained by the long workdays. He calls on the head monk uses his two words to say, "I'm leaving."

"Good," the head monk replies. "You've done nothing but complain since you got here."

Late one night a guy is showing some friends around his brand new apartment.

The last stop is the bedroom, where a big brass gong sits next to the bed.

"What's that gong for?" the friend asks him.

"It's not a gong," the man replies, "It's a talking clock."

"How does it work?"

The guy picks up a hammer, gives the gong an ear shattering whack and steps back.

Suddenly, someone on the other side of the wall in the next apartment screams, "For goodness sake, you jerk...it's 3:30 in the morning!"

"What time does the library open?" the man on the phone asked.

"Nine A.M." came the reply. "And what's the idea of calling me at home in the middle of the night to ask a question like that?"

"Not until nine A.M.?" the man asked in a disappointed voice.

"No, not till nine A.M.!" the librarian said. "Why do you want to get in before nine A.M.?"

"Who said I wanted to get in?" the man sighed sadly. "I want to get out."

A man walks into a bar, and orders a drink. As he sits there, the jar of nuts on the bar tells him what a nice shirt he is wearing. Disturbed by this, he reaches for the pay phone. As he approaches the phone, it starts screaming and shouting at him.

He runs to the bar and explains this to the barman. The barman apologizes and says, "The peanuts are complimentary, but the pay phone is out of order"!

Signs that you have grown up

1. Dinner and a movie is the whole date instead of the beginning of one.

2. You actually eat breakfast food at breakfast time.

3. Eating a basket of chicken wings at 3 AM now severely upsets, rather than settles, your stomach.

4. 6:00 AM is when you get up, not when you go to bed.

5. You hear your favorite song on an elevator.

6. You watch the Weather Channel.

7. Your friends marry and divorce instead of date and break up.

8. You go from 130 days of vacation time to 14.

9. Jeans and a sweater no longer qualify as "dressed up."

10. You're the one calling the police because those kids next door won't turn down the stereo.

11. Your car insurance goes down and car payments go up.

12. You feed your dog Science Diet instead of McDonald's leftovers.

13. Sleeping on the couch makes your back hurt.

14. You no longer take naps from noon to 6 PM!

.

A lady inserted an 'ad' in the classifieds: "Husband wanted".

Next day she received a hundred letters. They all said the same thing: "You can have mine."

The village blacksmith finally found an apprentice willing to work hard at low pay for long hours. The blacksmith immediately began his instructions to the lad "When I take the shoe out of the fire, I'll lay it on the anvil; and when I nod my head, you hit it with this hammer."

The apprentice did just as he was told. Now *he's* the village blacksmith.

Yes, this is a real book that I came across.

Q: How many artists does it take to change a light bulb?

A: Ten. One to change it, and nine to reassure him about how good it looks.

A man speaks frantically into the phone, "My wife is pregnant, and her contractions are only two minutes apart!"

"Is this her first child?" the doctor queries.

"No, you idiot!" the man shouts. "This is her husband!"

A housewife, an accountant and a lawyer were asked, "How much is 2+2?"

The housewife replies: "Four!"

The accountant says: "I think it's either 3 or 4. Let me run those figures through my spreadsheet one more time."

The lawyer pulls the drapes, dims the lights and asks in a hushed voice "How much do you want it to be?"

A woman and her little girl were visiting the grave of the little girl's grandmother. On their way through the cemetery back to the car, the little girl asked, "Mommy, do they ever bury two people in the same grave?" "Of course not, dear." replied the mother, "Why would you think that?" "The tombstone back there said 'Here lies a lawyer and an honest man.'"

"Doctor, Doctor, You've got to help me - I just can't stop my hands shaking!"

"Do you drink a lot?"

"Not really - I spill most of it!"

An applicant was asked if he was familiar with any machines. He said "Four." "That's great. What are the four machines?" He said, "Coke, coffee, candy, and cigarette."

After surgery, the surgeon told his patient: "I'm afraid we're going to have to open you back up. Because, you see, I forgot my rubber gloves inside you."

Patient: "Well, if that's all, I'd rather pay for them if you just leave me alone."

Doctor: "I have some bad news and some very bad news."

Patient: "Well, you might as well give me the bad news first."

Doctor: "The lab called with your test results. They said you have 24 hours to live."

Patient: "24 hours! That's terrible!! What could be worse?! What's the very bad news?"

Doctor: "I've been trying to reach you since yesterday."

Ladies, when a woman steals your spouse, there is no better revenge than to let her keep them.

"Doctor" said the patient, "are you sure I'm suffering from pneumonia? I once heard of a doctor treating someone with pneumonia -- and finally he died of typhus."

"Don't worry, that won't happen to me", the doctor replied. "If I treat someone with pneumonia he'll die of pneumonia."

A guy walks into work, and both of his ears are all bandaged up. The boss says, "What happened to your ears?"

He says, "Yesterday I was ironing a shirt when the phone rang and pshhhhh! I accidentally answered the iron."

The boss says, "Well, that explains one ear, but what happened to your other ear?"

He says, "Well, jeez, then I had to call the doctor!"

———————————————————————

The woman applying for work in a Florida lemon grove seemed way too qualified for the job.

Foreman: "Look Miss, have you any actual experience in picking lemons?"

Woman: "Well, as a matter of fact, yes! I've been divorced three times."

———————————————————————

Dear Christopher,

I know you joke about having A.D.D. so I thought I would email you about a condition I call A. A. A. D. D. - Age Activated Attention Deficit Disorder

This is how it manifests:

I decide to water my garden. As I turn on the hose in the driveway, I look over at my dirty ol' Pontiac and decide it needs washing. As I start toward the garage, I notice that there is mail on the porch table that I brought up from the mailbox earlier. I decide to go through the mail before I wash the car. I lay the car keys down on the table, put the junk mail in the garbage can under the table, and notice that the can is full. So, I decide to put the bills back on the table and take out the garbage first. But then I think, since I'm going to be near the mailbox when I take out the garbage anyway, I may as well pay the bills first. I take my checkbook off the table, and see that there is only one check left. My extra checks are in my desk in the study, so I go inside the house to my desk where I find the can of Diet Coke that I had been drinking. I'm going to look for my checks, but first I need to push the Diet Coke aside so that I don't accidentally knock it over. I see that the pop is getting warm, and I decide I should put it in the refrigerator to keep it cold. As I head toward the kitchen with the Diet Coke, a vase of flowers on the counter catches my eye--they need to be watered. I set the Diet Coke down on the counter, and I discover my reading glasses that I've been searching for all morning. I decide I better put them back on my desk, but first I'm going to water the flowers. I set the glasses back down on the counter, fill a container with water and suddenly I spot the TV remote. Someone left it on the kitchen table. I realize that tonight when we go to watch TV, I will be looking for the remote, but I won't remember that it's on the kitchen table, so I decide to put it back in the den where it belongs, but first I'll water the flowers. I pour some water in the flowers, but quite a bit of it spills on the floor. So, I set the remote back down on the table, get some towels and wipe up the spill. Then I head down the hall trying to remember what I was planning to do.

At the end of the day:

* the car isn't washed

* the bills aren't paid

* there is a warm can of Diet Coke sitting on the counter

* the flowers don't have enough water

* there is still only one check in my check book

* I can't find the remote

* I can't find my glasses

I don't remember what I did with the car keys.

Then when I try to figure out why nothing got done today, I'm really baffled because I know I was busy all day long, and I'm really tired. I realize this is a serious problem, and I'll try to get some help for it, but first I'll send Christopher an e-mail.

After a quarrel, a husband said to his wife, "You know, I was a fool when I married you." She replied, "Yes, dear, but I was in love and didn't notice."

Man is incomplete until he is married. Then he is finished.

A woman was telling her friend, "It is I who made my husband a millionaire."

"And what was he before you married him?" her friend asked.

"A billionaire" she replied.

The young lady, upon her engagement, went to her mother and said, "I've found a man just like father!" Her mother replied, "So what do you want from me, sympathy?"

A little boy asked his father "Daddy, how much does it cost to get married?" And the father replied, "I don't know son, I'm still paying."

I want to die in my sleep like my grandfather...not screaming and yelling like the passengers in his car...

Young Son: "Is it true, Dad, I heard that in some parts of Africa a man doesn't know his wife until he marries her?"

Father: "That happens in every country, son."

"I never knew what real happiness was until I got married; and then it was too late."

Q. What's the difference between a run over dog and a run over lawyer?

A. The dog has skid marks before it

A tourist asks a man in uniform, "Are you a policeman?"

"No, I am an undercover detective."

"So why are you in uniform?"

"Today is my day off."

The most effective way to remember your wife's birthday is to forget it once.

Teacher: "If you reached in your right pocket and found a nickel, and you reached in your left pocket and found another one, what would you have?"

Boy: "Somebody else's pants."

A policeman pulls a man over for speeding and asks him to get out of the car. After looking the man over he says "Sir, I couldn't help but notice your eyes are bloodshot. Have you been drinking?"

The man gets really indignant and says, "Officer, I couldn't help but notice your eyes are glazed. Have you been eating doughnuts?"

A policeman stops a lady and asks for her license.

Policeman: "Lady, it says here that you should be wearing glasses."

Woman: "Well, I have contacts."

Policeman: "I don't care who you know! You're still getting a ticket!"

One evening a man arrived home from work and found his wife waiting for him at the front door.

"I want you to take me somewhere expensive tonight," she said.

"No problem, honey," the man replied. " I know just the place."

"So," his wife asked as they were pulling out of their driveway, "where are we going?"

"The gas station," he replied

A woman's husband had been slipping in and out of a coma for several months, but she dutifully stayed by his bedside every single day. One afternoon, he finally opened his eyes. When he did, he looked at his wife and said, "You've always been with me through the bad times. When I got fired, you were there to support me. When my business failed, you were there. When I got hot, you were by my side. When we lost the house, you stayed with me, and when my health started failing, you were still by my side. So you know what?"

"What dear?" his wife asked, smiling bravely.

"I think you're really bad luck," he said.

A husband and wife were dining out together when the wife noticed that her husband kept staring at an attractive woman who was sitting at the bar throwing back drink after drink.

"Do you know that woman?" she asked.

"Yes," her husband replied. "She's an ex-girlfriend. She started drinking after we broke up, and apparently she hasn't been sober since."

"My goodness!" his wife exclaimed. "Who'd have thought a person could celebrate for that long?"

"Dad, can you write in the dark?"

"I think so. What is it you want me to write?"

"Your name on this report card."

Wisdom From My Grandmother

1. If you're too open minded, your brains will fall out.

2. Age is a very high price to pay for maturity.

3. Going to church doesn't make you a Christian any more than going to a garage makes you a mechanic.

4. Artificial intelligence is no match for natural stupidity.

5. If you must choose between two evils, pick the one you've never tried before.

6. My idea of housework is to sweep the room with a glance.

7. Not one shred of evidence supports the notion that life is serious.

8. It is easier to get forgiveness than permission.

9. For every action, there is an equal and opposite government program.

10. If you look like your passport picture, you probably need the trip.

11. Bills travel through the mail at twice the speed of checks.

12. A conscience is what hurts when all your other parts feel so good.

13. Eat well, stay fit, and die anyway.

14. Men are from earth. Women are from earth. Deal with it.

15. No husband has ever been shot while doing the dishes.

16. A balanced diet is a cookie in each hand.

17. Middle age is when broadness of the mind and narrowness of the waist change places.

18. Opportunities always look bigger going than coming.

19. Junk is something you've kept for years and throw away three weeks before you need it.

20. There is always one more imbecile than you counted on.

21. Experience is a wonderful thing. It enables you to recognize a mistake when you make it again.

22. By the time you can make ends meet, they move the ends.

23. Thou shalt not weigh more than thy refrigerator.

24. Blessed are they who can laugh at themselves for they shall never cease to be amused.

Where in the nursery rhyme does say that Humpty Dumpty is an egg?

Teacher: "Johnny, what is the outside of a tree called?"

Johnny: "I don't know."

Teacher: "Bark, Johnny, bark!"

Johnny: "Woof, woof..!"

So ya know, I've been taking these kung-fu classes lately. I must say they're great. They teach you how to be as powerful as a tiger, as quick as a monkey, as smart as a dragon. Just the other day, these guys came up to me with a knife and demanded money. So, I turned into a chicken and ran!

A man wrote a letter to a small hotel he planned to visit on his vacation: "I would very much like to bring my dog with me. He is well groomed and very well behaved. Would you be willing to permit me to keep him in my room with me at night?"

An immediate reply came from the hotel owner, who said, "I've been operating this hotel for many years. In all that time, I've never had a dog steal towels, bedclothes, silverware or pictures off the walls. I've never had to evict a dog in the middle of the night for being disorderly. And I've never had a dog run out on a hotel bill. Yes, indeed, your dog is welcome at my hotel.

And, if your dog will vouch for you, you're welcome to stay here, too."

A busload of tourists arrives at Runnymede. They gather around the guide who says, "This is the spot where the barons forced King John to sign the Magna Carta."

A fellow at the front of the crowd asks, "When did that happen?"

"1215," answers the guide.

The man looks at his watch and says, "Darn! Just missed it by a half hour!"

Teacher: "You know you can't sleep in my class."

Boy: "I know. But maybe if you were just a little quieter, I could."

A man on his deathbead made one final dying request of his wife.

"Darling, promise me you will marry Andrew after I'm gone," he said.

"Of course, honey, anything you want." His wife replied. "but I thought you hated Andrew."

With his last dying breath her husband said, "I do."

How do you make a blonde laugh on Saturday?

Tell her a joke on Wednesday.

The child comes home from his first day at school.

Mother: "What did you learn today?"

Kid: "Not enough. I have to go back tomorrow."

My twins even step up to help

during hard economic times.

A guy stood over his tee shot for what seemed an eternity, looking up, looking down, measuring the distance, figuring the wind direction and speed. Driving his partner nuts.

Finally his exasperated partner says, "What is taking so long? Hit the ball!"

The guy answers, "My wife is up there watching me from the clubhouse. I want to make this a perfect shot."

"Well, you don't stand a chance of hitting her from here!"

A brunette is trying to get across a river and suddenly she spots a blonde on the other side.

She yells over to the blonde "Hey, excuse me! How do I get over to the other side?"

After a quick survey of the river, the blonde calls back "You ARE on the other side!"

An English professor complained to the pet shop proprietor, "The parrot I purchased uses improper language."

"I'm surprised," said the owner. "I've never taught that bird to swear."

"Oh, it isn't that," explained the professor. "But yesterday I heard him split an infinitive."

Four People

This is a story about four people, named Everybody, Somebody, Anybody, and Nobody.

There was an important job to be done, and Everybody was sure that Somebody would do it.

Anybody could have done it, but Nobody did. Somebody got angry about this, because it was Everybody's job. Everybody thought Anybody could do it, but Nobody realized that Everybody wouldn't do it. It ended up that Everybody blamed Somebody when Nobody did what Anybody could have done!

Knowing that the minister was very fond of cherry brandy, one of the church elders offered to present him with a bottle on one condition... that the Pastor acknowledges receipt of the gift in the church paper.

"Gladly," replied the good man.

When the church magazine came out a few days later, the elder turned at once to the "appreciation" column. There he read: "The minister extends his thanks to Elder Brown for his gift of fruit and for the spirit in which it was given."

Two boll weevils grew up in South Carolina. One went to Hollywood and became a famous actor. The other stayed behind in the cotton fields and never amounted to much.

The second one, naturally, became known as the lesser of the two weevils.

I would give my right arm

to be ambidextrous.

The nice thing about being senile is you can hide your own Easter eggs.

Top 45 Oxymorons

45. Act naturally

44. Found missing

43. Resident alien

42. Advanced BASIC

41. Genuine imitation

40. Airline Food

39. Good grief

38. Same difference

37. Almost exactly

36. Government organization

35. Sanitary landfill

34. Alone together

33. Legally drunk

32. Silent scream

31. Living dead

30. Small crowd

29. Business ethics

28. Soft rock

27. Butt Head

26. Military Intelligence

25. Software documentation

24. New classic

23. Sweet sorrow

22. Childproof

21. "Now, then ..."

20. Synthetic natural gas

19. Passive aggression

18. Taped live

17. Clearly misunderstood

16. Peace force

15. Extinct Life

14. Temporary tax increase

13. Computer jock

12. Plastic glasses

11. Terribly pleased

10. Computer security

9. Political science

8. Tight slacks

7. Definite maybe

6. Pretty ugly

5. Twelve-ounce pound cake

4. Diet ice cream

3. Working vacation

2. Exact estimate

1. Microsoft Works

━━━━━━━━━━━━━━━━━━━━━━━━━━━━━━━━━━━━

A funeral service is being held for a woman who has just passed away. As the pallbearers are carrying out the casket, they accidentally bump into a wall. Hearing a faint moan from inside, the woman's husband opens the casket and finds that his wife is actually alive!

She dies again, 10 years later, at which point her husband has to go through another funeral. This time when the pallbearers carry the casket toward the door, the husband yells out, "Watch out for the wall!"

A couple drove several miles down a country road, not saying a word after an earlier discussion had led to an argument, and neither wanted to concede their position.

As they passed a barnyard of mules and pigs, the wife sarcastically asked, "Relatives of yours?"

"Yep," the husband replied, "In-laws."

Two old men in a retirement village were sitting in the reading room and one said to the other, "How do you really feel? I mean, you're 75 years old, how do you honestly feel?"

"Honestly, I feel like a newborn baby. I've got no hair, no teeth, and I just peed myself."

I wonder...

1. Why are there interstate highways in Hawaii?

2. What WAS the best thing before sliced bread?

3. What would chairs look like if our knees bent the other way?

4. If you choke a smurf, what color does it turn?

5. If you cross a four-leaf clover with poison ivy, would you get a rash of good luck?

6. What the world be like without theoretical questions?

7. If a no-armed man has a gun, is he armed?

8. If you got into a taxi and the driver starts driving backwards, does she/he owe you money?

9. If con is the opposite of pro, then is Congress the opposite of progress?

10. If you throw a cat out a car window, does it become kitty litter?

Three retirees, each with a hearing loss, were taking a walk one fine March day.

One remarked to the other, "Windy, ain't it?"

"No," the second man replied, "It's Thursday."

The third man chimed in, "So am I. Let's have a coke."

A man sitting through the first quarter of the Super Bowl can't help but notice the conspicuously vacant seat next to the man to the right of him.

Wanting to make polite conversation he leans over to the man and says "Can you believe someone paid all that money for a seat to the Super Bowl and then doesn't show up?"

The man turns to him and says, "That's my wife's seat she recently passed away." "Oh I am so sorry to hear that." the first man said, "didn't anyone else in your family want the Ticket?"

The second man never took his eyes from the football game, "Sure, they did, but they're all at the funeral."

Grandchildren don't make a man feel old ... it's the thought that he's married to a grandmother.

I had trouble with the idea of turning 30 and was oversensitive to any signs of advancing age. When I found a prominent gray hair in my bangs, I pointed to my forehead and asked my husband, "Oh no, have you seen this?"

"What?" he asked. "The wrinkles?"

There's this guy who had been lost and walking in the desert for about 2 weeks. One hot day, he sees the home of a missionary. Tired and weak, he crawls up to the house and collapses on the doorstep. The missionary finds him and nurses him back to health. Feeling better, the man asks the missionary for directions to the nearest town.

On his way out the back door, he sees this horse. He goes back into the house and asks the missionary, "Could I borrow your horse and give it back when I reach the town?" The missionary says, "Sure but there is a special thing about this horse. You have to say 'Thank The Lord' to make it go and 'Amen' to make it stop."

Not paying much attention, the man says, "Sure, OK." So he gets on the horse and says, "Thank The Lord" and the horse starts walking. Then he says, "Thank The Lord, Thank The Lord" and the horse starts trotting. Feeling really brave, the man says, "Thank The Lord, Thank The Lord, Thank The Lord, Thank The Lord, Thank The Lord" and the horse just about takes off.

Pretty soon he sees this cliff coming up and he's doing everything he can to make the horse stop. "Whoa, stop, hold on!!!! "Finally he remembers, "Amen!!" and the horse skids to a stop 4 inches from the edge of the cliff.

The man sinks slowly back into the saddle, sighs deeply, and lets out a heartfelt, " Thank The Lord"

Why didn't the lifeguard rescue the drowning hippie?

She was too far out.

While strolling on the beach, a man finds a golden lamp. Rubbing the lamp, he is suddenly confronted by a genii.

"I shall grant you three wishes, but keep in mind, your ex wife shall receive double your wish."

The man thinks carefully and then proceeds to ask for one billion dollars.

"Your wish is granted, plus, your wife in now the recipient of TWO billion dollars."

"Unhappy about this situation, the man thinks carefully and asks to be granted an extra one hundred years of life."

"It is done, and your wife shall now live an additional TWO hundred years."

Frustrated, the man looks the genii straight in the face, "I want you to scare me half to death."

———————————————————

A retired man who volunteers to entertain patients in nursing homes and hospitals went to one local hospital in Brooklyn and took his portable keyboard along. He told some jokes and sang some funny songs at patients' bedsides.

When he finished he said, in farewell, "I hope you get better."

One elderly gentleman replied, "I hope you get better too."

———————————————————

"I hold an OCD meeting at my house every second Tuesday. I don't have OCD, it's just a way to get my house cleaned for free."

———————————————————

A blonde wanted to go ice fishing. She'd seen many books on the subject, andfinally getting all the necessary tools together, she made for the ice.After positioning her comfy footstool, she started to make a circular cut inthe ice. Suddenly, from the sky, a voice boomed,

"THERE ARE NO FISH UNDER THE ICE."

Startled, the blonde moved further down the ice, poured a thermos ofcappuccino, and began to cut yet another hole. Again from the heavens thevoice bellowed,

"THERE ARE NO FISH UNDER THE ICE."

The blonde, now worried, moved away, clear down to the opposite end of theice. She set up her stool once more and tried again to cut her hole.The voice came once more,

"THERE ARE NO FISH UNDER THE ICE."She stopped, looked skyward, and said,"IS THAT YOU LORD?"

The voice replied,"No, this is the manager of the hockey rink."

_____

A couple goes out to dinner to celebrate their 50th wedding anniversary.

On the way home, she notices a tear in his eye and asks if he's getting sentimental because they're celebrating 50 wonderful years together. He replies, "No, I was thinking about the time before we got married.

Your father threatened me with a shotgun and said he'd have me thrown in jail for 50 years if I didn't marry you. Tomorrow I would've been a free man!"

———————————————————————————————

Two old men had been best friends for years, and they both live to their early 90's, when one of them suddenly falls deathly ill. His friend comes to visit him on his deathbed, and they're reminiscing about their long friendship, when the dying man's friend asks, "Listen, when you die, do me a favor. I want to know if there's baseball in heaven."

The dying man said, "We've been friends for years, this I'll do for you." And then he dies.

A couple days later, his surviving friend is sleeping when he hears his friend's voice. The voice says, "I've got some good news and some bad news. The good news is that there's baseball in heaven."

"What's the bad news?"

"You're pitching on Wednesday."

———————————————————————————————

Two old men are talking about their aches, pains and bodily functions.

One seventy-year-old man says, "I have this problem. I pee like clockwork at 7AM every morning."

The other old man says, "So what's your problem

"I don't wake up until nine."

A wise old gentleman retired and purchased a modest home near a junior high school. He spent the first few weeks of his retirement in peace and contentment. Then a new school year began.

The very next afternoon three young boys, full of youthful, after-school enthusiasm, came down his street, beating merrily on every trashcan they encountered. The crashing percussion continued day after day, until finally the wise old man decided it was time to take some action.

The next afternoon, he walked out to meet the young percussionists as they banged their way down the street. Stopping them, he said, "You kids are a lot of fun. I like to see you express your exuberance like that. In fact, I used to do the same thing when I was your age. Will you do me a favor? I'll give you each a dollar if you'll promise to come around every day and do your thing."

The kids were elated and continued to do a bang-up job on the trashcans. After a few days, the old-timer greeted the kids again, but this time he had a sad smile on his face. "This recession's really putting a big dent in my income," he told them. "From now on, I'll only be able to pay you 50 cents to beat on the cans." The noisemakers were obviously displeased, but they accepted his offer and continued their afternoon ruckus. A few days later, the retiree approached them again as they drummed their way down the street.

"Look," he said, "I haven't received my Social Security check yet, so I'm not going to be able to give you more than 25 cents. Will that be okay?" "A lousy quarter?" the drum leader exclaimed. "If you think we're going to waste our time, beating these cans around for a quarter, you're nuts! No way, mister. We quit!" And the old man enjoyed peace.

───────────────────────────────

A 60-year-old man went to a doctor for a check-up. The doctor told him, "You're in terrific shape. There's nothing wrong with you. Why, you might live forever; you have the body of a 35-year-old. By the way, how old was your father when he died?"

The 60-year-old responded, "Did I say he was dead?"

The doctor was surprised and asked, "How old is he and is he very active?"

The 60-year-old responded, "Well, he is 82 years old and he still goes skiing three times a season and surfing three times a week during the summer."

The doctor couldn't believe it. So, he asked, "Well, how old was your grandfather when he died?"

The paitient responded again, "Did I say he was dead?"

The doctor was astonished. He said, "You mean to tell me you are 60 years old and both your father and your grandfather are alive? Is your grandfather very active?"

The 60-year-old said, "He goes skiing at least once a season and surfing once a week during the summer. Not only that," said the patient, "my grandfather is 106 years old, and next week he is getting married again."

The doctor said, "At 106-years, why on earth would your grandfather want to get married?"

His patient looked up at the doctor and said, "Did I say he wanted to?"

━━━━━━━━━━━━━━━━━━━━━━━━━━━━━━━━━━━━━━

"Give me a sentence about a public servant," said the Mother helping her son at home.

The small boy wrote: "The fireman came down the ladder pregnant."

The mother took her son aside to correct him. "Don't you know what pregnant means?" she asked.

"Sure," said the young boy confidently. "It means 'carrying a child.'"

An 80-year-old couple were having problems remembering things, so they decided to go to their doctor to get checked out to make sure nothing was wrong with them. When they arrived at the doctor's, they explained to the doctor about the problems they were having with their memory.

After checking the couple out, the doctor tells them that they were physically okay but might want to start writing things down and make notes to help them remember things. The couple thanked the doctor and left.

Later that night while watching TV, the old man got up from his chair and his wife asks, "Where are you going?"

He replies, "To the kitchen."

She asks, "Will you get me a bowl of ice cream?"

He replies, "Sure."

She then asks him, "Don't you think you should write it down so you can remember it?"

He says, "No, I can remember that."

She then says, "Well, I also would like some strawberries on top. You better write that down cause I know you'll forget."

He says, "I can remember that, you want a bowl of ice cream with strawberries."

She replies, "Well, I also would like whip cream on top. I know you will forget that so you better write it down."

Irritated, he says, "I don't need to write that down,

I can remember that." He then fumes into the kitchen.

After about 20 minutes he returns from the kitchen and hands her a plate of bacon and eggs.

She stares at the plate for a moment and says, "You forgot my toast."

Two elderly women were out driving in a large car-both could barely see over the dashboard. As they were cruising along they came to an intersection. The stoplight was red but they just went on through. The woman in the passenger seat thought to herself "I must be losing it, I could have sworn we just went through a red light."

After a few more minutes they came to another intersection and the light was red again and again they went right though. This time the woman in the passenger seat was almost sure that the light had been red but was really concerned that she was losing it. She was getting nervous and decided to pay very close attention to the road and the next intersection to see what was going on.

At the next intersection, sure enough, the light was definitely red and they went right through and she turned to the other woman and said, "Mildred! Did you know we just ran through three red lights in a row! You could have killed us!"

Mildred turned to her and said, "Oh, am I driving?"

A rabbi was called to a Miami Beach Nursing Home to perform a wedding.

An anxious old man met him at the door. The rabbi sat down to counsel the old man and asked several questions. "Do you love her?"

The old man replied, "I guess."

"Is she a good Jewish woman?"

I don't know for sure," the old man answered.

"Does she have lots of money?" asked the rabbi.

"I doubt it."

"Then why are you marrying her?" the rabbi asked.

"She can drive at night," the old man said

Three ladies were discussing the travails of getting older. One said, "Sometimes I catch myself with a jar of mayonnaise in my hand, while standing in front of the refrigerator, and I can't remember whether I need to put it away, or start making a sandwich."

The second lady chimed in with, "Yes, sometimes I find myself on the landing of the stairs and can't remember whether I was on my way up or on my way down."

The third one responded, " Well, ladies, I'm glad I don't have that problem. Knock on wood," as she rapped her knuckles on the table, and then said, "That must be the door, I'll get it!"

With the average cost for a Nursing Home per day reaching $188.00,there is a better way when we get old & feeble. I have already checked on reservations at the Holiday Inn for a combined long-term stay discount and senior discount of $49.23 per night. That leaves $138.77 a day for:

1. Breakfast, lunch and dinner in any restaurant I want, or room service.

2. Laundry, gratuities and special TV movies. Plus, they provide a swimming pool, a workout room, a lounge, washer, dryer, etc. Most have free toothpaste and razors, and all have free shampoo and soap.

3. They treat you like a customer, not a patient. $5 worth of tips a day will have the entire staff scrambling to help you. There is a city Bus stop out front, and seniors ride free. The Handicap bus will also pick you up (if you fake a decent limp). To meet other nice people, call a Church bus on Sundays. For a change of scenery, take the Airport shuttle Bus and eat at one of the nice restaurants there. While you're at the airport, fly somewhere. Otherwise, the cash keeps building up.

4. It takes months to get into decent nursing homes. Holiday Inn will take your reservation today. And you are not stuck in one place forever, you can move from Inn to Inn, or even from city to city. Want to see Hawaii? They have a Holiday Inn there too.

5. TV broken? Light bulbs need changing? Need a mattress replaced? No problem. They fix everything, and apologize for the inconvenience. The Inn has a night security person and daily room service. The maid checks to see if you are ok. If not, they will call the undertaker or an ambulance. If you fall and break a hip, Medicare will pay for the hip, and Holiday Inn will upgrade you to a suite for the rest of your life.

6. And no worries about visits from family. They will always be glad to find you, and probably check in for a few days mini-vacation. The grand kids can use the pool. What more can you ask for?

So: As I reach the Golden age I'm facing it with a grin. I'll just check into the nearest Holiday Inn!

A man plays a game of poker with his friends every weekend. One evening he comes home after his game, and tells his wife to pack her bags, she is going to live with one of his poker buddies.

"What are you talking about?" she asks.

"I lost you to him in poker tonight, just pack your bags!"

"How could you lose me in a poker game," the exasperated woman asks.

"It wasn't easy; I had to fold with four aces."

Three elderly gentlemen were talking about what their grandchildren would be saying about them fifty years from now.

"I would like my grandchildren to say, 'He was successful in business'," declared the first man.

"Fifty years from now," said the second, "I want them to say, 'He was a loyal family man'."

Turning to the third gent, the first gent asked, "So what do you want them to say about you in fifty years?"

"Me?" the third man replied. "I want them all to say, "He certainly looks good for his age'!"

For the first time in many years, an old man traveled from his rural town to the city to attend a movie. After buying his ticket, he stopped at the concession stand to purchase some popcorn.

Handing the attendant $1.50, he couldn't help but comment, "The last time I came to the movies, popcorn was only 15 cents."

"Well, sir," the attendant replied with a grin, "You're really going to enjoy yourself. We have sound now."

Some thoughts from a retired mind

I was thinking about how a status symbol of today is those cell phones that everyone has clipped onto their belt or

purse. I can't afford one, so, I'm wearing my garage door opener.

You know, I spent a fortune on deodorant before I realized that people who avoided me just didn't like me.

I was thinking that women should put pictures of missing husbands on beer cans, and men should put pictures of their missing wives up at the mall!

I was thinking about old age and decided that old age is when you still have something on the ball, but you are just too tired to bounce it.

I thought about making a fitness movie, for folks my age, and call it "Pumping Rust."

I have gotten that dreaded furniture disease: That's when your chest is falling into your drawers!

I've come to realize that the secret to a happy life is not looking like Barbie or Ken and suffering through tofu and rice cakes to stay that way! It's eating chocolate, staying chunky and explaining that you're really a perfect size 6, but you keep it covered with fat so it doesn't get scratched!

I know, when people see a cat's litter box, they always say, "Oh, have you got a cat?" Just once I want to say, "No, it's for Visitors!"

Employment application blanks always ask 'who is to be notified in case of an emergency' I think you should write, "A Good Doctor!"

Why is it that every time I lose weight it finds me again?

Why do they put pictures of criminals up in the Post Office? What are we supposed to do -- write to these men? Why don't they just put their pictures on the postage stamps so the mailmen could look for them while they deliver the mail? Or better yet, arrest them while they are taking their pictures!

Just once, when someone says, "How are you?" (without really wanting to know), I'd like to say "Well, I can't keep my teeth in, I pee on myself every time I laugh, my hair is falling out, I cannot see where the heck I'm going most of the time, my back hurts and I pass gas every time I sneeze

(and feel like sneezing right now)! I'll bet that'd cure 'em from asking again!

━━━━━━━━━━━━━━━━━━━━━━━━━━━━━━━━━━━━━━━

A man and his bride are at a resort for their honeymoon. The resort offers horseback riding and they decide to give it a try. They start off down the trail, when a noise startles the bride's horse. It rears, jostling the bride. The groom jumps off his horse, grabs the reins of the horse, gets right into the horse's face, and says, "That's one!"

The couple rides a while longer. A flock of birds, startled by the horses, flies up out of the brush. Again, the bride's horse jumps back, and she bounces around in the saddle. The groom jumps off his horse, calms the bride's horse, look it in the eyes, and says, "That's two!"

Near the end of the ride, a rabbit runs in front of the couple. The bride's horse is spooked, and the bride falls from the saddle. The groom jumps off his horse, makes sure the bride is not injured, and then says to the horse, "That's three." He pulls out a gun and shoot the horse, killing it.

The appalled bride scream, "You are a sick man. You're a mean spirited and vicious human being! I can't believe that I married someone as heartless as you!"

The groom looks her in the eye and says, "That's one!"

My wife comes to the realization that we are

actually married.

THE NEW "OVER-40" BARBIES

1.) Bifocals Barbie. Comes with her own set of blended-lens fashion frames in six wild colors (half-frames too!), neck chain and large-print editions of Reader's Digest.

2.) Hot Flash Barbie. Press Barbie's bellybutton and watch her face turn beet red while tiny drops of perspiration appear on her forehead! With hand-held fan and tiny tissues.

3.) Facial Hair Barbie. As Barbie's hormone levels shift, see her whiskers grow! Available with teensy tweezers and magnifying mirror.

4.) Cook's Arms Barbie. Hide Barbie's droopy triceps with these new, roomier-sleeved gowns. Good news on the tummy front, too: muumuus are back! Cellulite cream and loofah sponge optional.

5.) Bunion Barbie. Years of disco dancing in stiletto heels have definitely taken their toll on Barbie's dainty arched feet. Soothe her sores with this pumice stone and plasters, then slip on soft terry mules. Colors: pink, rose, blush.

6.) No More Wrinkles Barbie. Erase those pesky crow's-feet and lip lines with a tube of Skin Sparkle-Spackle, from Barbie's own line of exclusive age- blasting cosmetics.

7.) Soccer Mom Barbie. All that experience as a cheerleader is really paying off as Barbie dusts off her old high school megaphone to root for Babs and Ken Jr. With minivan in robin's egg blue or white, and cooler filled with doughnut holes and fruit punch.

8.) Midlife Crisis Barbie. It's time to ditch Ken. Barbie needs a change, and Bruce (her personal trainer) is just what the doctor ordered, along with Prozac. They're hopping in her new red Miata and heading for the Napa Valley to open a B&B. Comes with real tape of "Breaking Up Is Hard to Do."

9.) Single Mother Barbie. There's not much time for primping anymore! Ken's shacked up with the Swedish au pair in the Dream House and Barbie's across town with Babs and Ken Jr. in a fourth-floor walk-up Barbie's selling off her old gowns and accessories to raise rent money. Complete garage sale kit included.

10.) Recovery Barbie. Too many parties have finally caught up with the ultimate party girl. Now she does 12 steps instead of dance steps! Clean and sober, she's going to meetings religiously. Comes with little copy of The Big Book, and a six-pack of Diet Coke.

SENIORS TEXTING CODES

ATD - At The Doctors

BFF - Best Friend Fell

BTW - Bring the Wheelchair

BYOT - Bring Your Own Teeth

FWIW - Forgot Where I Was

GGPBL - Gotta Go Pacemaker Battery Low

IMHO - Is My Hearing-Aid On

LMDO - Laughing My Dentures Out

OMMR - On My Massage Recliner

ROFLACGU - Rolling On Floor Laughing And Can't Get Up...

What Generation Are You?

Welcome to the generational assessment test. Note your answer to each of the following questions and review your results at the end.

Who is the ideal figure of motherhood?
A - Eleanor Roosevelt
B - Donna Reed
C - Mrs. Brady
D – Lois Griffin

What did you want to be when you grew up?
A - Part of a nuclear family
B - Someone who makes lots of money
C - Living with your parents
D - Living with your parents

Music should be:
A - Melodic and romantic
B - Annoying to your parents
C - Annoying to your parents
D - Annoying to your parents

The scariest moment in film history was:
A - When the mummy rose from his tomb
B - When the Blob chased Steve McQueen
C - When the alien burst from the man's chest
D – Watching any of the Twilight movies

The most inspiring American is:
A - John Wayne
B - John F. Kennedy
C - John F. Kennedy Jr
D – The boys of South Park

I expect my retirement to be:
A – When I can look back on a happy, fulfilling life
B - An opportunity to finally write my novel
C - An agonizing slide into abject poverty
D - A daily struggle to survive in a horribly polluted world

America is becoming:
A - More impersonal
B - More frightening
C - More expensive
D - Whatever

The American Dream is:
A - A house with a two-car garage
B - A healthy family
C - Winning the lottery
D - Touring with Justin Bieber

My college major was:
A - Business
B - Liberal arts
C - Secondary to my bartending job
D - Something far, far away

A good meal would be:
A - Meat and potatoes
B - Vegetarian macrobiotic
C - From a drive-up window
D - Microwaveable

My favorite footwear is:
A - Sensible shoes
B - Earth shoes
C - Converse high-tops
D - Doc Martens

I learned to drive behind the wheel of a:
A - '53 Packard
B - '61 VW
C - '78 Pinto
D – PS3

The "woman":
A - Marilyn Monroe
B - Raquel Welch
C - Julia Roberts
D – Megan Fox

The "man":
A - Cary Grant
B - Paul McCartney
C - Eddie Vedder
D – Ryan Reynolds

Lost idol:
A - James Dean
B - Jim Morrison
C - Kurt Cobain
D - Mario Bros

Fashion accessory best forgotten:
A - Double knit
B - Bell bottoms
C - Skinny ties
D - Ridiculously baggy pants

The best way to spend a weekend is:
A - Playing golf
B - Consciousness raising
C - Mountain biking
D - Internet surfing

I remember where I was when:
A - The Japanese surrendered
B - John F. Kennedy was shot

C - John Lennon was shot
D – Brad and Angelina got engaged

Life changing movie:
A - East of Eden
B - Easy Rider
C - Heathers
D – Anchor Man

Life-changing novel:
A - Catcher in the Rye
B - Fear and Loathing in Las Vegas
C - Bright Lights Big City
D – Vampire Diaries

Sports hero:
A - Mickey Mantle
B - O.J. Simpson
C - Michael Jordan
D - Tebow

Celebrity my generation would rather not claim:
A - Joe McCarthy
B - Barry Manilow
C - Vanilla Ice
D – Hannah Montana

Computers are:
A - Frightening and disconcerting
B - Complicated
C - Part of life
D - My only link to the outside world

The father is the one who:
A - Brings home the bacon
B - Is attuned to his sensitive side
C - Left years ago
D - Holds the remote control

My after-college plans:
A - Work hard to help build a strong America
B - Take my pick of many job opportunities
C - Take my pick of many low-paying temp services
D - Would you like fries with that?

My generation's most annoying fad is:
A - Nuclear testing
B - Hula hoops
C - Body piercing
D - Unemployment

The voice of my generation:
A - Walter Cronkite
B - Bob Dylan
C - Madonna
D – Kim Kardashian

My generation's biggest fear is:
A - Heart disease
B - Getting older
C - Collection agencies
D – Not getting likes on Facebook

RESULTS:

If you answer mostly A, you're a pre-boomer. If you answer
mostly B, you're a Baby-Boomer. If you answer mostly C, you're
in Generation X. If you answer mostly D, you're in Generation Y.

_____

Aging Is When...

1. *Everything hurts and what doesn't hurt, doesn't work.*

2. *The gleam in your eye is the sun hitting your bifocals.*

3. *You feel like the night after, but you haven't been anywhere.*

4. *Your little black book contains only names ending in M.D.*

5. *You get winded playing chess.*

6. *Your children begin to look middle-aged.*

7. *You finally reach the top of the ladder and find it leaning.*

8. *You join a health club, but don't go.*

9. *You begin to outlive enthusiasm.*

10. *Your mind makes contracts that your body can't keep.*

11. You look forward to a dull evening.

12. "25 Years Ago Today", is your favorite part of the newspaper.

13. You sit in a rocking chair and can't get it going.

14. Your knees buckle and your belt won't.

15. The best part of the day is over when the alarm clock goes off.

16. Your back goes out more often than you do.

17. You sink your teeth into a steak and they stay there.

18. You forget, why you are reading this.

A man is enjoying a late night drink when he notices that must have had too much fall from his stool. He runs over and puts him back on the stool, only to watch him fall again a few minutes later.

He feels sorry for the man and calls a cab after getting the man's address from his driver's license. The man has a terrible time making it to the cab, falling down three more times. The Good Samaritan decides it would be best to ride with the man to insure his safe arrival home.

The man stumbles and falls two more times from the cab to the front door.

Hearing a commotion, the man's wife opens the front door.

"Ma'am, I brought your husband home," the Samaritan exclaims.

"Thank you so much, but where's his wheelchair?" asks the wife.

———————————————————————————————————

Driving through a small town, a man comes to an intersection where the cross traffic has the right of way. Instead of coming to a full stop, he slows, notices a break in traffic and makes a right turn. No sooner had he turned than a cop puts on his lights and pulls the man over.

"You didn't stop at that intersection," says the cop.

"I know officer, but I did slow down," replies the man.

"Yes, but you didn't stop"

"No, but I slowed down."

"But you didn't stop," the cop angrily replies.

"No, but what is the difference really," asks the young man.

The cop takes out his nightstick and starts to hit the young man. "Now, what do you want me to do," he asks, "slow down or stop?

Submitted from a fan:

Today at the drugstore, the clerk was a gent.

From my purchase this chap took off ten percent.

I asked for the cause of a lesser amount;

And he answered, "Because of the Seniors Discount."

I went to McDonald's for a burger and fries;

And they're, once again, got quite a surprise.

The clerk poured some coffee, which he handed to me.

He said, "For you, Seniors, the coffee is free."

Understand---I'm not old---I'm merely mature;

But some things are changing, temporarily, I'm sure.

The newspaper print gets smaller each day,

And people speak softer---can't hear what they say.

My teeth are my own (I have the receipt.),

and my glasses identify people I meet.

Oh, I've slowed down a bit... not a lot, I am sure.

You see, I'm not old... I'm only mature.

The gold in my hair has been bleached by the sun.

You should see all the damage that chlorine has done.

Washing my hair has turned it all white,

But don't call it gray... saying "blond" is just right.

My car is all paid for... not a nickel is owed.

Yet a kid yells, "Old duffer... get off of the road!"

My car has no scratches... not even a dent.

Still I get all that guff from a punk who's "Hell bent."

My friends all get older... much faster than me.

They seem much more wrinkled, from what I can see.

I've got "character lines," not wrinkles... for sure,

But don't call me old... just call me mature.

The steps in the houses they're building today

Are so high that they take... your breath all away;

And the streets are much steeper than ten years ago.

That should explain why my walking is slow.

But I'm keeping up on what's hip and what's new,

And I think I can still dance a mean boogaloo.

I'm still in the running... in this I'm secure,

I'm not really old... I'm only mature.

Book 2: Laugh Yourself Well

Chapter 1: Laughter is the Best Medicine

"A clown works like an aspirin, only twice as fast"

-Groucho Marx

Is the day coming when your doctor will tell you to watch two episodes of a sitcom and call him in the morning? Maybe not, but more and more, humor is being recognized as a powerful force for maintaining good mental and physical health. The idea that laughter is good for you is nothing new, but now science is proving it.

"I always heard laughter is the best medicine. I remember when my sister broke her arm. I laughed and laughed. It's true, I felt so much better."

-Christopher James

Over the past two decades, the effects of humor on the physical, psychological and social levels have been taken very seriously. It appears that the humor experience has compelling and deeply rooted repercussions in human physiology. Medical researchers at a dozen or more medical centers have been probing the effects of laughter on the human body and have detailed a wide array of beneficial changes. Extensive experiments have been conducted; working with a significant number of human beings, showing that laughter contributes to good health. Scientific evidence is accumulating to support the biblical axiom that 'a merry hearth does good like a medicine.'

The ancient Greeks included a visit to the "home of Comedians" as part of their "therapies process" in their healing centers. Laughter is one of the four 'natural tranquillizers'. *Anatomy of an Illness* is an account by Norman Cousins of his experiences fighting a paralyzing and very painful illness, called ankylosing spondylitis, from which, specialists told him encouragingly, he had one chance in five hundred of recovery. Mr. Cousins is a remarkable man who wondered ... if negative emotions produce harmful chemical changes in the body, won't positive emotions like love, hope, faith, confidence and laughter produce chemical changes. This idea caused many doctors a lot of amusement.

Norman shows that there's now reason to believe that laughter counteracts panic and the effects of panic in seriously ill people, that it also works against the depression which itself inhibits the production of disease-fighting cells, and that laughter actually increases the number of immune cells in the body, including cells that fight some kinds of cancer. Cousins believed that endorphin's, the body's natural painkillers, are produced during laughter. Endorphin release would account for the pain relief and the feeling of being naturally 'high' that most people experience after a period of prolonged laughter. Studies show that there is a direct correlation between intensity of mirth and levels of catecholamine, hormones that cause the release of endorphins. There have been numerous examples that I have experienced where I have had high temperatures or been ill, and still have gone on to perform my comedy shows. While doing shows in Ohio I came down with a terrible case of pneumonia. I eventually found myself in the hospital and suffered through weeks of recovery. After being discharged I carried on with the tour, wondering if I was well enough to perform. What was interesting was that while I was performing there was no pain what so ever ... even then I knew my body was producing it's own natural pain killer, I just didn't know that they were called Endorphins

Through the use of humor and laughter you are giving yourself permission to self-heal. A quote of love is, "In life, what you resist persists." Humor can be a wonderful release for people, because if you deal with what's bothering you, in the very process of dealing with it, it will go away, and one of the best ways to deal with it is by using humor. Hearty laughter has a scientifically demonstrable exercise impact on several body systems; you could compare it to the effects of a physical exercise like aerobics. Mirthful laughter involves extensive skeletal muscle participation which Norman Cousins calls 'internal jogging'. When we have a good belly laugh our muscles are activated; heart race is increased; respiration is amplified with increase in oxygen exchange. Hearty laughter is followed by a state of compensatory physical relaxation, which lessens physical tension.

Having been involved with cancer patients, both children and adults, I have seen first hand how mirth can lift cancer-oppressed spirits, humor and depression are incompatible. With only the exception of the most severe degrees of depression, humor relieves the devitalizing grip of depression. It offsets, opposes, and diminishes depression. At times of tragedy, humans turn instinctively to comedy for it's depression-lifting effects. My grandmother's saying, "You can laugh or you can cry" is very apt to most people during depression. As a professional comedian I remember when the local economy was having hard times several years ago and yet I found myself with more work than before. Many industries and businesses had closed down in and around my home base of Youngstown, Ohio. I realized during those times that people used humor as a means of escape and to try and build their spirits up.

As a comedian, I have also taken my show to nursing homes with very gratifying results. Not only did I gain valuable experience that would serve me well in later years. Quite often I would get comments from the nurses that I made a person smile and brighten up who had not smiled since they were put in the home. The laughter wakes up some brain cells that may have been dormant for a long time, and that's healthy.

"Scientists say we only use 10% of our brain. Imagine if we could harness the other 60%!"

-Christopher James

So, laughter being the best medicine is more than a cliché. It does change cells, it is medicine, meditation and marvelous. When people are feeling depressed I always suggest they go to a hospital or home and try and cheer someone up ... it's amazing how therapeutic this can be for both parties.

On my office wall I had a notice by Dr. Donald Ardell that read: "Wellness is too important to be presented grimly, living a wellness lifestyle is fun, romantic, hip, sexy and free, and people who choose to live this way are stronger, better looking, have higher morale, superior bowel movements and more antibodies to resist illness. Humor is the soul of wellness. In order to live a wellness lifestyle, you can't always take life seriously."

The research on heart attacks also raises important ideas about how we can use laughter. It is interesting that humor opposes directly those emotions, which have been recorded as being associated with precipitation of heart attacks. The two emotions they discovered were fear and rage. Humor acts to relieve fear and rage is impossible when laughter and fun are present.

One of the greatest things about humor is that it is

creative. It pushes your brain, gets you thinking about elements of life in new ways, develops new insights, calls forth unexpected and ingenious associations, calls your attention to factors in an experience or situation which you hadn't previously noticed ... humor stirs up the cerebral neurons.

Dr. Kathleen M. Dillon, of Western New England College has added this to the research evidence on the salutary effects of laughter. She measured salivary immunoglobulin A (sIgA) concentrations in student volunteers before and after they viewed humorous and nonhumorous thirty-minute videotapes. Salivary immunoglobulin A is believed to have a protective capacity against some viruses. Dr. Dillon discovered that these protective concentrations increased significantly after the students viewed the humorous videotape. The concentrations remained unchanged after the nonhumorous tape. She also found that the individuals who said they turned to humor as a way of coping with difficult life situations also had the highest initial levels of the protective concentrations. Her conclusion was that a consistently cheerful approach to life boosted the body's disease-fighting forces. She replicated this finding in a study of nursing mothers.

According to the December 1989 issue of The American Journal of Medical Science, hearty laughter may be helpful in preventive and the healing process. The article was written by Lee S. Berk, DHSc, MPH, Assistant Research Professor of Pathology and Laboratory Medicine at Loma Linda University School of Medicine and was co-authored by Stanley A. Tan, MD, PHD; William F. Fry, MD; Babara J. Napier; Jerry W. Lee, PhD; Richard W. Hubbard, PhD; John E. Lewis, PhD and William C. Eby, MD, PhD.

Dr. Berk says that this study "has shown objective, measurable, and significant neuroendocrine and stress hormones changes with mirthful laughter that suggest a physiological benefit. Laughter is a form of stress", Dr. Berk says. "We believe that laughter is a beneficial stress and that it conforms to the concept of something that Dr. Hans Selye called eustress - or good stress".

The carefully controlled study conducted by Dr. Berk and his colleagues has provided data that mirthful laughter can decrease or attenuate classical stress hormonal responses. Stress hormones usually increase during distress, or bad stress.

"Our data showed that serum cortisol, growth hormone and plasma dopac decreased with laughter, plasma epinephrine was lower in the experimental laughter group, and serum prolactin, beta-endorphin, adrenocorticotrophic hormonte (ACTH) and plasma norepinephrine did not significantly increase."

Dr. Berk notes that a "positive or happy outlook gives one more edge in the patient's behalf. Removing helplessness and replacing it with hopefulness do seem to have a place in healing. I don't think a positive attitude is going to be a panacea where you think yourself well. However, I think it can be part of the total preventive or therapeutic package."

In a more recent study which was conducted in 1996, Dr. Berk and Dr. Stanledy investigated the effects of eustress, related to mirthful laughter, on interferon-gamma (IFN), an immunoregulator. IFN is a lymphokine, a soluble product produced by some lymphocytoses that exert numerous biological functions including a variety of specific and nonspecific effects on other cells. IFN is produced by activated T cells and natural killer cells. It is active in fighting viruses and regulating cellular growth. Its capacity, however, to regulate or modulate immune properties is believed to be its most important quality. Gamma interferon serves to ensure cooperation between certain cells in the adaptive immune response. It interacts with other cytokines in either a synergistic or antagonistic manner.

They concluded that, "The precise role of IFN in human diseases and therapy is not clearly understood. However, we know that it is clearly involved in the defense against parasites, viruses (intracellular pathogens), and possibly tumor cells. It is interesting to note that new gene therapy approaches in cancer show promise in immunomodulation for the induction of antitumor effects. Chiron Viagene, an immunology technology company, has developed two retroviral vectors for gene therapy of cancer, one of which is IFN Retrovector. Direct injection of IFN Retrovector results in significant tumor regression in several syngeneic mouse tumor models. Additionally, treatment with IFN Retrovector enhances antitumor cellular lytic activity in mice, yielding complete tumor regression. This finding clearly demonstrates its potential effectiveness. A separate but related point is that a deficiency in the production of gamma interferon has also been related to persistent viral (EBV) infections. He concludes by saying, "Since many of these substances are capable of modifying immune components, these changes in neuroendocrine and stress hormones during behavior manipulation may turn out to play a significant role in immunomodulation - that is, changing the immune system for the better".

Dr. Berk then goes on to say, "As medical scientists, we must express considerable caution relative to drawing conclusions. However, when combining the results of this research with our previous studies, an interesting pattern appears to emerge. As mentioned earlier, our initial investigations have shown that mirthful laughter is a positive stress or "eustress" phenomena. It is associated with activation of T cells, B cells and increases in immunoglobulins and natural killer cell activity. It is well known that IFN plays important roles in the growth and differentiation of cytotoxic T cells, activation of NK cells and functions as a B cell maturation factor (B cells are responsible for making immunoglobulins). Based upon this understanding, it is reasonable to propose that there indeed may be a correlative relationship (at a molecular level) between the presence of IFN and other components of the immune system. Further research, however, is necessary to elucidate these effects on the composite immune response."

What all this is telling us is that although stress is inevitable and necessary in life, the negative effects of stress do not have to be inevitable. Good Stress is a balance of arousal and relaxation that helps you concentrate, focus, and achieve what you want. Bad Stress is constant stress and constant arousal that may lead to high blood pressure, cardiovascular disease, and worse.

"I laughed so hard I fell off my seat"

No doubt you've heard this saying somewhere or it may have even happened to you. The above quote actually makes more sense that most people realize. When we have a good hearty laugh our entire muscular system relaxes, our body relaxes and goes limp. If you're sitting on a chair and you have a good belly laugh chances are that you may very well laugh yourself on to the floor.

Laughing For the Health of It

Think about spending a large percentage of your emotional day feeling negative. Think about spending most of your time around people who spend most of their lives being negative. It's not difficult to imagine a sinking, unhealthy response. Overexposure to negativity can make you feel sick. I believe it depletes your strength, making it more difficult for you to resist disease. Negative emotions might include anger, boredom, loneliness, depressed, shocked, hostile, defeated, frightened, guilty, sad, ignored, and hurt.

Now think about spending most of your day with people who relish the delectable dozen of positive emotions. It gives you a lift just thinking about it.

155

Exposure to an abundance of positivity can make you feel well. Positive emotions add a certain quality that enhances every aspect of life. Positive emotions might include joyous, calm, hope, cheerful, love, bountiful, kind, delighted, peaceful, happy, vivacious and affectionate.

"Laughter is a symbol for all of the positive emotions" Laughter enhances every aspect of life and is a symptom of health and well being. It is a way of getting off the downward spiral of negativity. Try the following exercise: Think back and remember people you have really liked. Name them and list their qualities. (Include relatives, friends, teachers, co-workers, and general acquaintences.

I'll bet you mentioned "sense of humor" as one of the qualities attributed to most of the people you like. Humor isn't for everyone. It's for people who want to enjoy life and feel fully alive. Many times after a performance, I'll have audience members visit me in the lobby. Occasionally, I will have a well meaning audience member say, "I usually can't stand comedy, but I loved your show." I'm often puzzled by this remark and try to imagine any person that simply doesn't like to laugh.

Laughter won't prevent us from dying in the long run, but it may increase life expectancy. It certainly adds to the quality of life. If positive emotions are healing, we should be getting as much as we can.

What things do you do that you consider to be healing activities?

Ask yourself this question: "What do I still want to do before I die?"

Well, what are you waiting for?

The Twelve Affirmation's

of Positive Humor

1 I am determined to use my humor for positive, playful, uplifting, healing and loving purposes.

2 I will take myself lightly while I take my work in life seriously.

3 I will not seek to be offended by other's attempts at humor. When in doubt, I will see others as meaning well.

4 I will express my humor physically, using my face and (when so moved) with my entire body.

5 I refuse to use my humor to camouflage hostility or prejudice.

6 I understand that the gift of laughter is a treasured gift, so I will laugh generously at other's attempts to be humorous.

7 All teasing and ethnic humor will be by mutual

consent and will go both ways or I will not engage in such humor.

8 I will respect the forbidden subject topics of my listeners. I will avoid giving offence with my humor.

9 If I offend another by my use of humor, I will make amends.

10 I will be eternally vigilant for the jokes and absurdities of the universe, and I will share my observations with my companions in life.

11 In the midst of adversity, I will continue to use my humor to cope, to survive, to heal, to grow, and to pass on loving-kindness.

12 On the day of my death I will look back and know that I laughed lovingly, fully and well.

Chapter 2: The Psychology of Laughter

What makes us laugh? Theories on the physiological origin of laughing have been put forth for centuries, but there has been no inclusive definitive answer found. Sigmund Freud thought laughter originated with the smile of an infant falling asleep at the breast - the emotional expression of pleasurable satiety.

Grades of Laughter

The medicine of the soul, or the sound of its

healing, is laughter. A wonderful experiment can be done by simply retreating to a safe environment and starting to laugh, and continuing to laugh, on and on for as long as one can stand it. The laughter, which begins forced, becomes genuine and torrents of secondary creations of various kinds shows up and dissipate. Laughter itself can also be a secondary creation; nervous or cynical or compulsively gleeful or destructive laughter form a range of social "offenses" between beings, or signals, which modulate the meaning of spoken language. Laughter can be assessed and measured against the heart's concerns and interests. Laughter comes in many forms that take the shape of a staircase.

The steps are:

1. Silent laughter, the laugh you have to yourself, a chuckle.

2. Smiles appear on the face together with crinkles and laughter lines.

3. The first sounds appear as chuckles and giggles ... the titter.

4. The volume grows and wry laughs, laughing along with someone.

5. Relief laughter

6. Belly laughs

7. Unrestrained hilarity.

Consider the sharp bark of the incredulous that knows that nothing is possible; the scornful and hopeless snort which while seeming to be a laugh, is actually a blowhard.

There is the sluggish whisper of the grief-lover, who laughs only to show regret.

The grimy laughs of the sadistic, and the slimy snicker of the covertly destructive, are laughs that stand out as false as a cigarette advertisement.

The terror-stricken laugh: a desperate whinny. The angry soul laughs with a kind of despotic glee, the laugh one gives when he is about to erase the tribe of his enemies in a psychotic frenzy. The laugh of the earnest battler is more like a rebel yell, a brave whoop of triumph or challenge.

There is also a kind of resigned sigh of laughter that is offered by the bored, the whisper of Indifferent Else where-ness.

More in tune with the business of creating is the chuckle of interest, a genuine laugh of those comfortably engaged in what they are doing. This is often found in the vicinity of the Snort of Surprise and the Chortle of Delight, all of which are sincere, solid laughs with no deception in their bellies.

The Chortle of Delight often gives rise to the Happy Belly Laugh, a gale of wonderment and recognition, that thrives wherever Truth invades the Land of Resisted Shadows. These are all found wherever consciousness is nurtured by the presence of sunlight and strong interest in the future.

The being who has found many opportunities for laughter often acquires a taste for the Clear Breeze of Enthusiasm, a rolling, light, happy laughter that never quite dies away even when the owner is asleep.

Higher still on the endless ladder is the Quiet Soul Laughter of Sheer Action. Its quietude is the intensity of all laughter without resistance, thus needing no noise to permeate its surround. The Serene Smile of Flawless Intent is similar, only tranquil to the depths of all being.

Another interesting fact is that when we laugh the brain's pleasure centers are tickled which are connected to our perceptions. A swift shift or switch in our perceptions can cause us to feel pleasure, crack a smile and even laugh out loud. I had the chance to witness this first hand two weeks ago. Some friends and I went to see the Australian Body Language expert Alan Pease who gave a talk on humor and was discussing his latest book on jokes. At the end of the talk, I bought a copy of the book and showed it to my two friends. On page 24 their was a picture that when viewed one way looked like a person reaching out with their hand, yet when it was turned upside down it became something entirely different, in this case it became something very rude. The quick shift in those people's perceptions caused unrestrained hilarity. On that picture alone my friends both bought a copy of the book!

A 'perception' is the meaning or understanding that our mind gives to the information reaching it. For example, your eyes might see a small black object. It is your mind that decides whether it is a wallet, a checkbook or an iPod. In the Alan Pease example above, we had difficulty seeing both of the pictures at the same time; it would only work if we turned it upside down. As a comedian I relate this by not giving away punchlines too early. The best jokes trigger the switch at the very last word.

Do you remember the feeling when somebody

tells you joke and then finally you are given the punchline, quite often there is that, "Oh, of course!" Research shows us there is a physical reaction when a punchline is solved. Using brain scans, researchers have been able to watch the physical movement as great punchlines shift the brain activity from one hemisphere to the other. One moment we are thinking left-brain 'logic', and the next our right hemisphere 'creativity' is flooded with electrical activity.

Children and Humor

Why are adults so serious, why are we so uptight? I think I know the reasons. Have you ever watched children when they are laughing? They know how to give belly laughs, and they will often laugh at anything. They are able to look at the littlest things and see the humor in it. If I were asked to describe children I would use adjectives like, playful, fun loving, wild, creative and spontaneous. If I had to describe an adult I would use words like, professional, serious, reserved, business like. We see those as appropriate types of behaviors, so when we see adults enjoying themselves and having fun in the workplace we question it.

Children have a lot to teach us, if we are open to learning from and with them. Children can also enlighten us by inviting us to lighten up. Have you ever seen a small child whose out of character behavior immediately brightens your day? I remember sitting in a restaurant a few years ago watching a small child at a neighboring table. This tiny human, relaxing in a high chair, was perfectly mimicking those at the table. Every facial expression, every hand movement, was a perfect reflection of the accompanying adults that were paying no attention to the child. The actions were so out of context, I immediately started laughing and could not stop for the remainder of the meal. This simple scenario made for a great evening and immediately changed the mood.

According to Dr. David Cohen, a British psychologist, laughing begins at a very early age. Most babies start to chuckle by the time they're only 9 weeks old, some when they're as young as 29 days. At first, a surprise or bodily sensation triggers laughter in the infant. At 4 to 6 months of age, touch and sound usually produce giggles. By 10 months, the baby laughs at something visually provocative, such as a funny face. When infants are about a year old, they begin to initiate their own laughter by playing games such as hide-and-seek or pretend falling down. How often do young children laugh? Cohen goes on to say that by age 16 weeks, babies laugh about once an hour; and by the time children are 4 years old - when they absolutely love slapstick - laughter breaks out on the average of every four minutes.

There is an excellent book called The Optimistic Child by Martin E.P Seligman, PH.D. which is about a revolutionary approach to raising resilient children. While he doesn't mention the word humor, he does talk about "an atmosphere of warmth and ebullience, clear safety signals, unconditional love but conditional praise, and lots of good events which all add positivity to the life of a child". Obviously humor can be included in many of these things. He goes on to say that "it is amazing however, for a child to be surrounded with good things and yet still have a gloomy mental life. What really matters, in the end, is how much positivity there is inside his or her little head."

A study by Greg Garamoni and Robert Schwartz, two University of Pittsburgh Psychologists, did a study to count the number of good thoughts and bad thoughts that different people have and to look at the ratio. They counted thoughts in many different ways: memories, reverie, causal explanations, and so on. Using twenty-seven different studies, they found that depressed people had an equal ratio: one bad thought to one good thought. Nondepressed people had roughly twice as many good thoughts as bad thoughts. This idea is literally simple-minded, but it is a powerful one. "It is also supported by the results of therapy: depressed patients who improve move to the 2:1 ratio from their original 1:1 ratio. Those who do not get any better stay at 1:1." It is possible by using humor to help ourselves and our children have a 2:1 ratio of good thoughts to bad thoughts.

Believe it or not, there was a period of time when I worked as a substitute public school teacher. I would observe how it was a struggle for some children to survive in school and after school around the neighborhood due to teasing. They try to survive by being better than the other kids at whatever they were doing. Little children don't like to be teased because they're trying so hard to be perfect. And yet, all of a sudden as you get older, you discover that the people who can laugh at themselves and accept some teasing are really some of the nicest people and the most popular of all. It would be nice if you could teach a small child not to be bothered by teasing when s/he starts off in school, and to realize how totally harmless it really is if you just don't pay any attention to it. But, of course, it can destroy you if you take it too seriously. It can ruin your entire childhood. I'm sure we all have a phrase or a comment thrown out by a peer, friend, or teacher that has stuck with us over the years.

A tough sense of humor, a bitter wit or sense of cynicism, can get you through hard times. As long as you keep people laughing, you maintain a certain protective distance. And as long as you keep laughing, you don't have to cry.

Humor Therapy

Branko Bokun advocates the need for humor therapy in 'cancer, psychosomatic diseases, mental disorders, crime, interpersonal and sexual relationships.'

Bokun argues in his book 'Humor Therapy' (published by Vita Books) that the brain is also a gland,

and that its glandular activity can be manipulated by thoughts or ideas created by the brains mental activity. The author blames the mentality of the adolescent male that pervades our society for resulting in high emotional arousal, 'inquietude, uncertainty and the fears of isolated and lonely individuals.'

Humor therapy helps us to realize that both unhappiness and gloom are infectious. 'That is why the pursuit of personal happiness only acquires a realistic meaning if it becomes the pursuit of other people's happiness.'

Bokun proposes humor courses, to help restore our inborn disposition towards playfulness, joy of living, curiosity, exploration and flexibility. His suggestions include:

-Develop a sense of self-ridicule, for instance by talking to oneself in the mirror.
-See amusing and happy films and plays, and read humorous books and magazines.
-Dedicate a corner of one's home to toys, as the mere sight and feel of them lessen tension.
-Hang pictures of children and animals on the walls

rather than staid or gloomy ancestors.

-Find a hobby, but change it the moment it is taken over-seriously. Preferably choose a hobby that cannot go against nature's harmonies, such as sailing or gardening.

-Have a pet and talk to it.

-See life through a haze of analogies to memorized jokes and anecdotes.

-Repeat three times every morning 'I am not the center of the universe'.

-Remember the eleventh commandment 'thou shalt not take thyself too seriously'.

Chapter 3: Destress With Humor

Stress is an inescapable part of modern life. That's the bad news. The good news is that stress isn't altogether bad news. In metered doses, it can be helpful, it can even make you better at what you do, and help give you the competitive edge. It's the full on all-out stress that is bad for you, and quite literally it can kill you.

In his book Stress without Distress, H. Selye

clarified that a person's interpretation of stress is not dependent solely on an external event, but also depends upon their perception of the event and the meaning they give it; — how you look at a situation determines if you will respond to it as threatening or challenging.

Because different people respond differently to the same environmental stimuli, some people seem to cope with stress better than others. Sociologist Suzanne Kobassa has defined three "hardiness factors" which can increase a person's resilience to stress and prevent burnout: — commitment, control, and challenge. If you have a strong commitment to yourself and your work, if you believe that you are in control of the choices in your life (internal locus of control), and if you see change as challenging rather than threatening; then you are more likely to cope successfully with stress. One theme that is becoming more prominent in the literature is the idea that a causative factor in burnout is a sense of powerlessness.

In this context, humor can be an empowerment tool. Humor gives us a different perspective on our problems and, with an attitude of detachment; we feel a sense of self-protection and control in our environment. As comedian Bill Cosby is fond of saying, "If you can laugh at it, you can survive it."

It is reasonable to assume that if locus of control measures strongly as internal, that a person will feel a greater sense of power and thus be more likely to avoid burnout.

What is Stress?

Stress is an adaptive response. It's the body's reaction to an event that is seen as emotionally disturbing, disquieting, or threatening. When we perceive such an event, we experience what one stress researcher called the "fight or flight" response. To prepare for fighting or fleeing, the body increases its heart rate and blood pressure; more blood is then sent to your heart and muscles, and your respiration rate increases. This response was probably beneficial to our cavemen ancestors who had to fight off wild animals.

But today, stress itself has become the "wild animal." Untamed and allowed to run rampant in our lives, it can destroy our health.

The modern male's response to psychological stress differs little from the way our primitive forebears reacted to dangerous animals or other sources of potential physical harm (i.e., with surges of adrenaline, a rise in blood pressure and heart rate, and a 4x increase in blood flow to the muscles needed to fight or run away).

Our stress response is more likely triggered by overwhelming responsibilities at home or work, by loneliness, or by the fear of losing our jobs.

What happens when we are stressed?

When you're feeling overwhelmed — or encounter a major stressor of some kind in your environment — your adrenaline kicks in and your sympathetic nervous system takes over. Your body is suddenly prepared for action. But when there's no dinosaur to slay or damsel in distress to rescue, your body reacts with heart palpitations, sweating, increased stomach acidity, stomach spasm, skeletal muscle spasms - and increased blood pressure. This is OK up to a point, but if it goes on too long and your body doesn't have any "down time," you could be in for trouble. Researchers tell us that stress may play a role in the development of high blood pressure, though more studies are necessary to tighten up the connection. Stress also appears associated with heart disease, even if a direct causal relationship has yet to be proven.

Stress is not bad in and of itself. It may help to make us more alert, energize us, or give us a motivational kick in the pants. For years, actors, entertainers, public speakers, and athletes have known how to turn stress into "high energy" performances. Properly harnessed, stress can indeed work to our advantage at times. Personally, I can relate to this many times over. I have been in performance situations that are less than ideal. I arrive to a venue that is clearly not a good fit for my show, whether it is the lighting, organization of the seats, stage size, or other factors. In some cases, it seems like the wrong situation for my show. These situations often lead to some of my most memorable and dare I say, best, shows of my career.

Enjoy the comedy show...

Occasionally, introductions to the stage are less than ideal. The host, ceo, or emcee, has little or no experience with such matters. They are not accustomed to introducing a comedian or are suffering from stage fright. I'm often reminded of an introduction that beyond bad.

I was booked to perform for a large church. As they didn't have a stage, I was to perform in the actual church hall. After carefully setting up my show, I huddled behind the alter, waiting for my introduction. The audience filed in from their buffet dinner and the minister took the stage. All started well and then he announced that he had a serious announcement. Apparently, the church secretary of 30 odd years had a relapse of a terminal disease and did not have much time left. He asked the audience to bow their heads as he led them in a very touching and heartfelt prayer. From behind the alter, I could hear sobs from the audience. Through tears, the minister then announced, "Our thoughts will be with the entire family, now my friends, enjoy the comedy show."

A somewhat less than ideal situation to be sure. I proceeded with the show, trying not to focus on the introduction. After the show, the church secretary stopped me and very emotionally thanked me for making it a special evening. What could have been a very morose and somber evening had been her chance to laugh and be with those that mattered the most in her life. I'll never forget that evening or how hard I worked to provide at least a little bit of healing.

Now, a whole field of research and study has

blossomed to investigate the relationship between psychosocial events and the immune system. It's called psychoneuroimmunology. Its proponents think that stress is involved, in some way, in the suppression of the immune system, which protects us from disease.

If stress is associated with immunosuppression, then stress management techniques should be useful in preventing, or at least tempering, the impact of stress on health. Certainly, stressors in life may sap our resistance and put us at greater risk for disease.

Humor is like an inner massage providing a priceless ability to relax in the face of tragedy, irritation, and disappointment. A well-placed laugh brings us out of today's crisis to break the stress cycle and return to productive-solving. Humor can help us re-frame stress into opportunity, humor and depression are incompatible.

What causes stress?

Major causes of stress include illness, job changes, moving, separations and divorces, deaths in the family, and financial difficulties. But even joyous events, like marriage, the arrival of a baby, or entertaining guests, can be stressful. When I ask people what stresses them the most, they always relate their stress to work. People seem to put a lot of pressure on themselves at work. Humor in the workplace is not taking work seriously; it's about taking yourself lightly and your work seriously.

At work change can often cause resistance and stress. Not all resistance is bad; it needs to be honored, listened to, and dealt with. Normal resistance can be handled by interjecting humor to keep people laughing at their uncomfortableness. Instead of creating more defensiveness, humor allows a blending with "complainer", defusing the situation. Humor also provides a support that gives people confidence that things are going to be fine, that the changes can be managed, a feeling of faith in the future. Laughter reduces anxiety, and so it helps people cope with the stress of change.

Lack of communication can also build up unwanted stress. We live in an entertainment age; if you do not find a way to keep your conversation interesting, people may tune you out. Effective communicators balance substance with style; they can be serious and humorous. Effective humor unlocks people's receptivity hence lessons stress; it also provides a memory hook for association to important information. If humor and laughter increased in organizations the amount of feedback a manager would get, the honesty and the capacity for people to say good things would rise. All the solutions to problems which lead to stress in organizations are within your own people, but the problem is half of them don't want to say anything, because they usually get knocked down. When you have self-esteem and things in perspective, you can laugh at yourself and your foibles.

"Managing for profit or bottom-line only is like playing tennis with your eye on the scoreboard and not on the ball".

Through my programs in humor advising, I do come across people who wonder, "what on earth I'm talking about, we need to get down to the bottom line, let's cut out the funny business". One concept we learn at school was the difference between process and product. Product is the end result, what you are trying to accomplish, while process is how you go about doing it and the interaction. People who keep on saying, "let's get back to business" are forgetting about the whole process.

How can humor be used to defuse anger?

An unexpected response can break the emotional tension and help move both people to problem solving. Humor can break down the anger cycle, but you will still need to listen and deal with the issue at hand. The safest focus of humor is yourself. Being able to laugh at oneself does not mean self-depreciation; it can be an acceptance of your own humanness. Laugh at what you do, not who you are, and the world will laugh with you. Only the self-confident can admit their mistakes;

183

humor helps us let go of our errors and move on.

"The richest laugh is at no one's expense"

-Nancy Loving

The use of negative humor in the workplace can be harmful. If you've ever been the butt of a joke or when people say to you, "I was only joking, can't you take a joke?" then you will know that some people use humor as a negative weapon. Humor is a powerful tool. How can you tell the difference between constructive and destructive humor, between humor that helps and humor that hurts, between "laughing with others" and "laughing at others"? In order to develop an effective sense of humor, we need to develop sensitivity to humor. This can be done by drawing a line between "laughing at others" and "laughing with others", risk interrupting toxic humor and finally by setting an example.

A list of humor that can be put downs include ethnic jokes, insults and toxic humor. These can create tensions between people and destroy teamwork; work against a persons self-esteem and reflect on the perpetrator's own self-concept and sense of security; reinforce stereotypes which are not true; minimize risk-taking, learning and creativity, invite retaliation and a focus on personalities and backfire, reflects anger, creates a cruel, abusive and offensive atmosphere.

From my experience as a comedian I have developed a style which doesn't rely on put-downs, racist or sexist humor. There have been tests, and I can confirm these from my experiences, that show people are likely to act in accordance with the model to which they have been exposed. Very rarely do I get people heckle me because I don't invite that type of humorous response from people.

While I do have fun with the situations my audience members are put into, I remain the butt of the joke. When people are "laughing at others" they are often being sarcastic, offending others, reinforcing stereotypes by making a single group the "butt" of the joke, destroying confidence and is usually based on contempt and insensitivity.

When people are "laughing with others" they are reducing tension by joking about human frustrations and faults which often leads to positive communication, encouraging people to relax and laugh, involves people in the fun and play, builds confidence and is based on caring and empathy, and creates a supportive atmosphere of fun and caring.

I would imagine that people who use negative humor in the workplace just aren't aware that it can be hurtful to others and eventually themselves. Their response is often, "Can't you take a joke?" They just aren't aware that this type of humor is hurtful. In my work I make people aware by being assertive, firm and taking risks. If you really want to kill a joke ask the person to explain it, this will definitely kill the joke and hopefully make the joke teller become aware that it wasn't funny.

Mental Health

Mental health is the ability to keep things in proportion. And what is a sense of humor but a sense of proportion.

Below is some advice to help with keeping things in perspective and ultimately helping relieve any stress.

1. Feeling Good About Yourself: Feeling low and useless as though you've hit rock bottom can be good because it means you're already at the bottom and is a chance to take stock of yourself. Invest some time in appreciating yourself first, because the more you appreciate yourself, the more your self will appreciate.

2. Less self-criticism: Self-criticism leads to a build up of self-doubt and worthlessness. Whatever it is you feel the urge to criticize yourself about, turn it into an appreciation of a positive trait. Give yourself credit for acknowledging a failure. Turn a negative into a positive. If you are being self-critical then don't look on it as a bad thing, be thankful you can acknowledge where you are.

3. Make friends with your inner-child: Most of us are so busy with being adults we leave the inner child at home whenever we go anywhere.

4. Laugh at least Once a Day: Laughter opens up to let life's experiences flow throughout you. Open up to laughter and humor. You don't have to be a funny person or a comedian to appreciate the benefits of humor. There is humor all around us, take the step to enjoy it and go with it.

Ways To Cope With Stress

Bill your doctor for time spent in his waiting room.

Fill out your bank deposit slip using Roman Numerals.

Have fun putting random items in other people's shopping carts

Lie on your back eating celery; using your navel as a salt dipper.

Make up a language and ask people for directions in it.

Pay your electric bill in pennies.

Put your toddler's clothes on backwards and send him to preschool as if nothing is wrong.

When someone says, "have a nice day", tell him or her you have other plans.

Chapter 4: Humor at Work

A sense of humor is an attitude and attitudes are learned. We can change old ones and develop new ones. Psychologists say that people are motivated toward the fulfillment of basic needs. Meaningful work provides an avenue for satisfying many of our needs. Most people work because they have a need to pay their bills, they want to socialize with others, be recognized for a job well done, and function to their full potential.

The ideal workplace provides us with enough money to help us feel secure, enough challenge and recognition so we feel like we are valued, and the opportunity to interact positively with others. Part of this positive interaction at work requires that you take your job seriously and yourself lightly.

There are two types of applications of humor. There is internal humor, you with yourself, and external humor, you with others. Generally speaking, you need to develop your internal humor before you can move to humor with others. Like many things, we have more humor in us than we realize, but it needs to be actively developed. To gain from humor, it needs to be approached with a spirit of fun and the inner child in us all. A good way to start appreciating humor is to be an observer and a listener. This will help you to improve your abilities to size-up situations and actively put your humor ideas to work. It will also enable you to see how others use humor successfully.

10 reasons humor benefits you, your organization and your customers.

1. Humor is a good motivator. No one will enjoy all parts of a job, but looking at the funny side will keep the harder parts palatable. The least expensive benefit in any job must be humor. It can also be one of the most important, it should never be a crime to have fun on a job. During stressful times morale at work can take a beating. When morale is low productivity goes down. It has been said that a 15% increase in morale can result in a 40% increase in productivity.

2. Humor generates creativity - it greases the wheel for creativity.

3. Productivity can increase when humor abounds. Difficult jobs are made easier.

4. Humor builds rapport and can break down barriers

5. Innovation thrives when humor is present. Any time stress can be reduced, when the pressure can be released, innovation will thrive.

6. It makes your organization more approachable and helps build customer relations.

7. As a training or teaching tool, humor is one of the best. Using humor to network or promote products is ideal and innovative. I am currently working on a book showing people how to use humor to network and get more

business.

8. People enjoy being around a person who is fun. One fun person can boost the spirits of a team of people, one fun person can give a place a boost of energy.

9. You can laugh or you can cry. Laughter is the best medicine.

10. Humor is a sign of health. Having a good sense of humor, being able to laugh at yourself and at a difficult situation is indicative of a good attitude.

Humor is:

-Creative, healing, the youngest feeling, the oldest reaction.

-Very important to survival and growth as a healthy human being.

-Ability to see human-ness of all of us by poking fun at certain human traits.

-Humility. In the face of sadness, despair, poverty we can hope and laugh at ourselves, self-understanding. It teaches us we are not as smart as we think, but we are capable of becoming smarter.

-Provide us with hope, optimism, perspective, joy and energy.

-A major instrument in developing insight, establishing and maintaining positive therapeutic rapport.

-Humor offers an alternative to violence. Wit, satire,

caricature and irony are available instead of bloodshed, murder and destructive violence. Humor teaches and reveals new understanding, humor at least gives us a choice.

-Humor is who we are. If your organization lacks humor, it is inhuman, it is taking something very special away from people. If humor is suppressed, other personal characteristics which are required to do business are also likely to be suppressed; in particular, mental health, job satisfaction and creativity.

Humor in the office

Laughter takes us back to a childlike (not childish) playfulness and spontaneity, which is inherently enjoyable. It is very freeing and gives us a sense of power when things around us seem out of control.

I am constantly amazed at some of the stories I hear from managers and employees regarding humor at the workplace. There are many stories where people are told that laughing with co-workers is inappropriate and that the use of humor with employees diminishes a manager's authority.

People who think along these lines are missing out on a powerful tool for improving people-handling skills. As discussed, when humor is used appropriately, it can help resolve conflicts, open communications, relieve office tensions and promote teamwork.

After years of working with executives, I am convinced there is a direct correlation between a sense of humor and effective administrators who use it to illustrate points, add color to meetings and spice up memos.

According to Mike Mescon, chairman of the department of management at Georgia State University, you can learn to become aware of the untapped resources in humor and to adapt them to your particular personality and management style. "If humor is just a facade", says Mescon, "it won't be effective."

Mescon's opinion is supported by a survey conducted by Richard J. Cronin for his executive search firm in Rosemont, Illinois. "Significantly, the corporate CEO's almost to a man, agreed that humor in business is healthy and important to the conduct of business; executives should develop a greater sense of humor in conducting business activities, and all other qualifications being equal, they would hire the job applicant with a better sense of humor ... I think the more secure you are, the more effectively you will use humor."

Psychiatrist Mel Udel agrees. "When I was an officer of Metropolitan Life Insurance Company, the most effective managers I knew always used humor. It's a good business strategy - in negotiating, for example - to disarm people. And it can also improve the work atmosphere in your office." Udel finds humor especially effective in defusing anger and lessening tension.

Many people associate intentional humor with giving speeches, where it can be quite effective.

It is a good idea to always be listening out for funny stories to build up a mental file of usable humor. In a speech the goal is not simply to be funny but to use relevant humor to drive a point home and to illustrate a problem, and most importantly to humanize the speaker.

I can never stress enough ... HUMOR IS GREAT FOR BUSINESS. Often the serious person doesn't take risks for fear of rejection or disapproval. In a business setting, this attitude can be counterproductive. I have this theory that if there was more fun in the workplace there would be less absenteeism.

Lack of employee loyalty can be a major problem in the business world - especially in the area of commission sales where turnover is traditionally very high. Humor can creep into everything from conversations, weekly sales letters to memos. Humor can be a tonic, and a constructive pressure valve allowing a person to criticize without hurting feelings.

Humor is not the only answer and will not cure everything, and does not fit everybody's style, although anyone can be humorous if the humor is adapted to one's personality. A person who is low-key needs understated humor. If you are not a funny person and feel uncomfortable making people laugh, you can work on developing a humorous personality - the ability to take one step back, put a situation in perspective, and see the funny side of it.

Workers who find the funny side of daily routines improve morale and increase cooperation. Humor can help turn around enemy relationships; we see a different side of them and they of us. Laughter is contagious and so is negativism. Which would you prefer?

My suggestion to people who want to develop their humor vision is to spend about 5 minutes each day standing back from things and just observing everything around you to get a perspective on what is happening. Look for the humor within you and around you. When you look for humor, humor finds you. If you were to imagine that you were filming a scene from Candid Camera and you have a camera in hand for 5 minutes, you will be amazed at how much humor you can capture around you. To develop your sense of humor call upon your other senses. Be farsighted and humor will introduce itself to you.

It is important that people take their jobs seriously, and themselves lightly. There is a difference between being a serious professional and being a solemn one. Hard work and humor go hand in hand.

How successful managers suggest view humor in the workplace:

1 It is essential to do a good job and still enjoy what you are doing.

2 My job involves interviewing people, humor plays a large part in relaxing the interviewee.

3 Laugh at yourself, so others can laugh at themselves with ease if something goes wrong. Because humor is so personal, and because people are so sensitive to the consequences of their attempts at humor, it's often safest to make fun of yourself. This makes it harder for someone to take offence. Self-deprecating humor is often interpreted by others as an expression of self-confidence.

4 Remember ... a full time job is only part-time in your life. Keep perspective with humor.

5 Encourage laughter on the job.

6 If you have a smile on your face, other people will smile.

7 Do not use humor at the expense of another or else it will backfire.

8 Looking at the environment, this tends to program us to push the laughter and joy deeper inside until it's hard to find.

9 Humor is made from pain, not pain inflicted by laughter.

10 Know thy people. Shakespeare wrote: "A jest's prosperity lies in the ear/Of him that hears it, never in the tongue/Of him that makes it". What is funny to one person may be a social statement to another. Get to know the people you work with and help them to know you.

11 Use humor to diagnose. Because humor can be so revealing, I use it to diagnose the character of a person and of their organization. In my advising to companies, I always pay attention to the kind of humor I hear.

We need to look beyond job satisfaction to bring the best out in people, both in terms of their productivity and mental health. Looking at children we can see joy and seemingly endless creative energy and enthusiasm. As adults we probably feel those feelings of fun every now and then, but not as often as we'd like. We can look at our educational and work institutions to see why these feelings are discouraged, they are very rarely rewarded. On top of that, many people view the world as a very serious place, a place in which it's hard to find fun.

From my work with companies and individuals I have discovered the power of humor. When the feelings of fun can be brought into the workplace, they have the potential to make the organization stronger. Making organizations fun may actually be a good investment.

Is it OK to have fun at work?

Yes!! There are three elements which lead to having fun at work. Firstly are the people's intentions, then the organization's culture or environment and finally the management behaviors.

People who try to make work fun have more fun at work. This may seem obvious and very simple on the face, but this effort by people who do use humor at work is based on a complex set of personal beliefs.

People who believe that fun has positive effects in their lives are more likely to try to make their jobs fun. Other people feel that fun doesn't belong at work and so it doesn't have positive effects. These people are less likely to attempt to make work fun, and they're less likely to have fun at work.

Imagine if everyone at your work took as their personal mission statement "to practice joy on the path of service." If you can create an atmosphere of trust and support in your company, where people can honestly say that "the happiness of others is our own business", then you will have created a sense of team where personal jealousies and office politics have far less meaning.

The idea that "If I'm having fun I can't really be working comes from the old Listerine management model: "it has to taste bad to be effective". Work has to feel like work or it really isn't work. If it feels good it must be play, or something worse.

In reality, people who enjoy their work say they cannot tell the difference between their work and their play - it feels so much the same. To be passionate about something means to love it. Some people love their work, can't wait to get there, and they do more of it than people who dislike or feel indifferent toward their work.

Choose a job you love and you will never have to work a day in your life.

-Confucius

People who are passionate about their work are also passionate in the rest of their lives. They love to play. They know that meaningful work, a positive attitude, and a joyful perspective on life make us healthier, happier, more productive, and more fun to be with.

I have witnessed many times the power of humor in the workplace. Perhaps the best example was when I toured with a company, which hired my services to help promote a new series of products. I have worked for many companies travelling the country with similar projects, but never have I experienced such a rapport with a company and it's clients than I had with this one. The Sales and Marketing Manager has a great sense of humor and was able to use it to his advantage many times over. We travelled for about a month giving the presentation every night, and at the end of the night the clients were all saying how they have never been to such a fun presentation such as this one.

For what is normally something that can be boring, the use of humor was used to great advantage to help people concentrate and keep them focused. It was also used to make points, how can they forget when it was announced a new brochure was to be introduced I came out saying these are the hottest tapware brochures around and it burst into flames. The relationship between the managers and the employees was one of respect simply because the employees knew how fortunate they were that both managers had a sense of humor and weren't scared to show their staff they were human. Laughter and play and fun on the job can help create a culture of caring and connection in the workplace that is just as important than productivity and profitability. The organization that laughs together stays together.

The organization's environment and management behaviors are also important to employee's fun. Managers may try to create an atmosphere of fun but they themselves need to follow it through. When employees see the management having fun and pursuing these goals, employees find their work to be more fun.

From my observations fun is not the same thing as job satisfaction. Having fun in work and being satisfied with work are two different things. Although employees might be satisfied with their jobs, it isn't enough, the work might not be fun. Once you begin incorporating fun into your work, you discover that the deeper purpose for doing so is to help create a genuine sense of job satisfaction for yourself as well as others.

There are of course those jobs which can be harder than others to create fun. This doesn't mean that there can't be fun in them, quite often people haven't stepped back and taken a look at how to have fun. Again, both employee and management behaviors are important to building fun in seemingly "fun-less" jobs.

There are times when it is inappropriate to play around at work, these include:

Not Funny - humor that detracts from the business at hand. When a group is moving in a forward direction and everyone is getting down to business and on with the task, humor that sidetracks the group is inappropriate.

When Humor ignores appropriate criticism or feedback - sometimes you'll laugh off criticism or feedback and that is just an indication that you are not taking your job seriously. Telling jokes for jokes sake is not always a good use of humor. Being a professional comedian is different from humor in the workplace. If you are always saying, "I've got a joke", you are setting yourself up to be funny. People are thinking, "OK, I'm going to here a joke so it better be funny".

When humor is insensitive to the group - You need to consider who you are around. There are many instances where industry specific humor is right on target. Lawyers can joke about lawyers, funeral directors about funeral directors and so on.

Sarcastic Humor - if somebody comes to work and has just brought a new suit and you say, "Wow, that will be nice when it comes back in fashion." Sometimes the off the wall, flippant humor just doesn't work.

Let humor be sensitive to the group, let it be a way to build rapport, put people at ease. Let it be a way of expressing the truth in a non-threatening way. In a meeting for example, keep it brief and to the point, actually use humor to make a point. Use it to illustrate a point.

Earlier I looked at children and humor and discussed what happens between childhood and adulthood, why is our humor often suppressed. As children we are told to "be serious" and "don't be so silly". I think that sometimes we are afraid of what others will think of us at work if we act a little silly now and then or show a sense of humor. Maybe we won't be taken seriously; we won't be treated with respect.

There does need to be a balance to counteract the seriousness in our lives and at work and a good way to balance it is to use humor.

For many of us, our best friends are those who can

reveal their true selves - including their silliest side and their sense of humor. I know that when people laugh at my humor or laugh at me being a goofball I feel great. Why? Because humor, especially silliness, reveal a very childlike and personal part of myself. In fact, the part that may be most fundamentally me, a part which has remained unchanged since my childhood. So when another person shows pleasure by laughing with me, the implicit message is, "I really like the real you." The natural high that I get from going up on stage and doing a show where everyone is laughing is just incredible, as I mentioned, this is my buzz and why I don't need to take drugs or drink. There is scientific evidence that shows also drugs can reduce a persons sense of humor.

Here are four types of funny people:

a) **Those who say funny things:** They tell jokes but are only as good as their material. Most of the skill is in the preparation of finding and remembering good stories.

b) **Those who say things funny:** These people get laughs from things not intrinsically funny. They use proper timing, dramatic voice inflections, and gestures to turn ordinary stories into hilarious monologues. They often rely on painful experiences shared playfully.

c) **Those who say funny things funny:** These people combine the first two, using good material told well.

d) **Those who think funny and who paint funny pictures in the minds of their listeners:** Their active imaginations are constantly tuned in and receptive to the humor others overlook. The world provides an inexhaustible supply of material for those who think funny.

Company Picnic Awards

This company had a picnic day which most employees went to. In the newsletter the following week appeared these awards which caused a great laugh at the office.

-Most Sunburnt Award

-Ugliest Sunglasses Award

-Most Enthusiastic Volleyball Player

-Split Trousers Award

-Best Volleyball Serve Award

-Late-Comer Because I got lost Award

-Best Tropical Outfit Award

-Best Family Uniform Award

How to incorporate humor and fun at work.

1. The first thing is to look at the people involved in your organization. Not everyone is the same in the way they like to get praise or acknowledgment. You need to ask who these people are, how do they have fun, what is funny to them? The more you know them the more effective you can be in using fun for reward, praise and acknowledgment.

2. It is important that management get in behind the idea of creating humor and fun at work. There is an old saying that says, the three best ways to lead are by example, example, and by example.

3. Your vocation should be a vacation. If you get great satisfaction out of your job then you are more likely to build up a good sense of team spirit. Feeling good about your work is very important. If you don't like your job and feel you are not getting personal satisfaction from it then you're in the wrong job. As

managers take time to enjoy employee's achievements and personal goals, this will help in connecting everyone together as a team and is important in developing long-term emotional wellbeing.

4. Don't rush things. Change takes time. It will take careful planning but the work will pay off. This includes introducing ideas and also getting staff used to the idea that they can enjoy themselves at work and have fun. There will be the stigma that if fun is introduced then "professionalism" flies out the window. Start slowly giving people time to feel comfortable with the idea that the company is learning to enjoy itself and to openly appreciate its employees.

HOW TO USE HUMOR IN PRESENTATIONS

1. Do use humorous stories and jokes which relate directly to the topic of your speech.

2. Don't laugh at your own story or joke.

3. Don't offend. For example: a person without a limb may not think a one-armed paperhanger joke is funny.

4. Do make the joke clear and to the point.

5. Do relate the story or joke to the audience.

6. Do speak audibly.

7. Don't repeat a story or joke that flops.

8. Don't repeat a story or joke that works.

9. Do tell a story or joke about yourself.

10. Do use the name of living persons in a story or joke to which the audience can relate.

Chapter 5: Creativity and Humor

"Humor and creativity can feed each other"

-Steve Allen

I was always in the mind that creativity depended on the possession of a special talent which someone was born with, but I have recently changed my view on this and discovered that it is possible to switch into the 'creative mood'.

In the seventies, some research was done by MacKinnon at Berkley which showed that highly creative people were no different in intelligence from those who seemed less creative; but that they took longer to study problems and that they "played with them more" … so the difference was that the highly creative knew how to switch themselves into a playful mood. In fact, MacKinnon describes this creative mood as being "more childlike." Humor is of course very close to childlike playfulness.

From my experiences as a humor advisor, I have discovered that comedy loosens up thinking and establishes an environment in which people can be creative. Humor stretches your thinking and you are forced to combine ideas that are usually not associated with one another. An example of this would be the person who combined a surfboard with a sail and wheels to get the sand surfing board. By combining things together and being creative they invented a new leisure activity.

The idea of humor is to take things lightly. If you are able to make fun of something, then you are likely to challenge the rules that give "something" it's legitimacy and even think of alternatives. By applying the same set of rules that make up humor such as asking "what if" questions, parodying the rules, breaking set, and apply it to problem solving, then you are likely to come up with fresh new approaches.

While humor may not solve every problem, it will sure put you in a more constructive frame of mind to do so.

The environment in the workplace is very important, if it's fun then it will be more productive. People who enjoy what they do will come up with more ideas. Countless psychology tests have found that many people think the best way to get along is to go along. Whenever people get together there is the danger of everyone of 'going along'. It has to do with people wanting the approval of the others rather than to come up with creative solutions to the problem at hand.

In his book, The Practice of Creativity by George M. Prince he says creativity is an unexpected astonishment, a vital triviality, a disciplined freedom, a familiar surprise, an intoxicating steadiness, a predictable initiation, a difficult delight and a demanding satisfier. George M. Prince used these compressed conflicts to describe "creativity", but they also describe humor. My conclusion is that humor and creativity are connected on a conceptual level.

From my personal experiences I believe that if you want to develop your sense of humor, one way is to nurture your creativity. Humor and creativity give us perspective, enlarge our boundaries, generate energy and help us lighten our lives.

In this time of rapid and unrelenting change, employees and employers are looking for ways to help themselves and their employees to cope more effectively. A sense of humor and joy in living can help us through times of change and crisis. We know that if we want to incorporate something new in our workplace we need to do it gradually, starting with small steps. If you ease into the idea of having fun at work and slowly help to spread it throughout your workplace, you will be surprised at how quickly people will pick up on the idea.

Healthy humor is vital to our well being and our ability to adapt to change.

Appropriate use of humor is a skill that can be learned. When we are learning any new skill, we start with small steps. First increase your own comfort level. Find out what things are funny for you and start to share that fun with others. Test the waters; see what kinds of things work for you and what things would be well received where you work. Take your cue from others when you are trying to be funny and see how it goes. If you sense that others are feeling uncomfortable, change your material or approach. It's OK to ask for feedback when you are using humor, to see if others are comfortable. Before long they will be joining the fun. Ideas on combining humor and creativity

Look at the world through the eyes of a three year old, a five year old or a baby. The sense of wonder that children have is at the heart of creativity. I discovered how powerful this could be when I started children's magic shows at the beginning of my career. When I became the magician I was able to see things through the eyes of a five year old, this ability shifted into my 'normal' life and I am able to laugh and enjoy life a whole lot more since. If you listen to children they ask a lot of funny questions, if you give yourself permission to ask such questions about things you will bring to life your creativity and humor.

Grab the bull by the horns and try out new ideas, be daring ... even if it's a step at a time. Find your comfort zone and then gradually and slowly push yourself half a step in the direction of risk. From here your creativity and humor ability will grow.

Creativity and humor often need to be warmed up before you can get straight into it; after they are warmed up they become energy generators. Use humor to start your engine of creativity and watch it flow.

I am often involved in creative meetings with various people in my business and always we end up laughing so much I have to leave the room, but out of this have come some very creative concepts. Rather than put down an idea as soon as it has been made, I try to think of at least three good things about the idea, this invites synergy and a contagion of laughter.

Be a kid again...

-Give yourself a gold star for everything you do today

-Grow a milk moustache

-Have a staring contest with your cat

-Make a face the next time somebody tells you "no"

-Ask "Why?" a lot

-Have someone read you a story

-Wear your favorite shirt with your favorite pants even if they don't match

-Do a cartwheel in public

-Hide your vegetables under your napkin at a

restaurant

-Make a "slurpy" sound with your straw when you get to the bottom of a milkshake

-Stick your head out the car window and moo if you see a cow

-Walk barefoot in wet grass

-Make cool screeching noises every time your car turns

-Count the colors in a rainbow

-Take a running jump over a big puddle

-Giggle a lot for no real reason

-Do that tap-someone-on-the-shoulder-while-you-stand-on-their-opposite-side-and- they-turn-around-and-no-one's-there thing

Chapter 6: The Full Time Comedian

"Who is the more foolish: the fool, or the

fool who follows him?"

-Obi Wan Kenobi, Star Wars

With my career choice as a professional comedian has come new ways to look at how humor can benefit the workplace, and in many ways I see myself like the King's court jester, the Corporate Fool. I am a professional advisor, the confidant, and the observer. Outside the court, free of in-house politics and promotion and favor, the Fool is in the best place to see things as they really are and to offer alternative perspectives. If the King wants honest answers such as "How do things look, really?" it is the fool he turns to. The Fool asks awkward questions like "Why?" and "Why Not?"

The jester has evolved quite a bit since 1202. He's become a far more abstract figure. His court has come to stand for a place of mirth and frivolity, a place to temporarily set aside the trials of life. There are now just as many jester she's as he's. Teenagers all over the country wear the jester's motley hat, whether they can juggle and sing or not. Simply being a funny person is reason enough to assume the jester's mantle. Why so many more jesters than clowns? Could be just etymology, but most people would agree that the jester has a certain nobility in his buffoonery that a clown lacks.

The word jester conjures a lot of things to mind. These days, the image that tends to jump to mind first is an oddly noble, frivolous, jocular fellow. Due to the sweeping range of his history, the jester has become extremely abstract, and several different, unique "types" of jesters have arisen. Here's just a sampler of a few that I've noticed:

The "look, -I-own-a-jester's-hat" Jester: This not necessarily jocular fellow is best noted for his often out-of-place jester's hat. Often a teenager, he doesn't necessarily know how to juggle or sing, and may just wear the hat for the nonstandard fashion statement it makes, or because he thinks he's funny. Though not "fake" jesters, there are certainly more sincere jesters out there.

The poor-but-wise "Shakespearean" Jester: Notable for their nonstandard clothes (for a jester), these guys are usually historically authentic, or at least they try to be. They don't go in for really gaudy hats or clothes, and aren't necessarily frivolous either. They often sing and make subtle humor, so they're not really raucous, but they do have an admirable authenticity about them.

The stereotypical "I'm probably a copyright by

now" Jester: This is the guy with the big goofy grin and hat with bells. He juggles and wears checkered tights, just like every good jester should. The "Stuffy" shirt corporation is probably trying to get the exclusive rights to him as we speak.

The "mystical-warlock-from-beyond" Jester: A purely modern creation, this jester came into being partly as a result of the jester's mysterious, noble aura, and partly as a result of the jesters image being used everywhere, often in fantasy and D&D-style pictures. Likely from another dimension, this jester wields fantastic and mysterious magical powers and doesn't do a lot of clowning.

The "Straight-out-of-Spawn-comics" Jester: A variation of the mystical jester, this guy is a total glamorization. He has James Bond refinement, a ridiculous number of points in his hat, and the ability to juggle obscene numbers of objects. Usually draw with dramatic perspective, he can do things most jesters only dream of.

The Professional Fool

I see myself as a modern day fool advisor. Don't be fooled by a professional fool. It takes intelligence, imagination, cleverness, and insight to play this role. The fool was consulted by Egyptian pharaohs and Babylonian Kings. His opinion was sought by Roman emperors and Greek tyrants. He advised Indian chiefs in the Pueblo, Zuni, and Hopi nations. He played an important role at the courts of the Chinese emperors. The fool was prominently employed by European royalty in the Middle Ages and Renaissance. Because of his ability to open up people's thinking, the fool has been held in as much esteem as the priest, the medicine man, and the shaman.

The fool had the license to parody any proposals under discussion and to shatter the prevailing mindset. The fool's candid jokes and offbeat observations put the issue in a fresh light and forced the king to reexamine his assumptions. By listening to the fool, the king improved his judgment, enhanced his creativity, and protected himself from going along with everyone else.

The fool lives and works by two key principles:

1. The Fool sees things as they really are

2. The Fool says things as they really are.

We can all be fools, we can balance our expertise and experience with honesty and innovation, if we follow these four principles:

1. Fools offer outside perspectives:

We often mix with people who are like us. We generally debate issues with those who already think like we do. A fool can offer an outside perspective that can generate new ideas and spark energy and creativity.

2. Fools see it like it is:

The Fool is able to see things as they are, no worse, no better ... just the way it is.

3. Fools are honest:

Out of seeing things as they are, comes honesty.

4. Fools are masters of communication:

Nobody will be grateful to you if you prove that they have to change - you have to persuade them to want to change - and that is a communication issue. This requires the skills of listening, understanding and building rapport and the tools of passion and energy.

The benefit of the fool's antics and observations is that they stimulate your thinking. They jolt your mind in the same way that a splash of cold water wakes you up. You may not like the fool's ideas, some of them may seem too way out, too silly or useless. But s/he forces you to entertain an alternative way of looking at your situation. The fool's approach to life jars you into an awareness that there is a second right answer to what you're doing, and that you should look for better answers than the ones you've got.

"But the fool on the hill sees the sun going down and the eyes in his head see the world spinning round."

-The Beatles

Over 120 ways to have fun at work.

- Set up a bulletin board in your room that has on the cartoons, funny photographs, jokes or humorous quotes related to the topic at hand. Encourage employees to contribute work related funny items

- Court gesture: on a rotating basis, have different people assume the role of " court gesture" in your meetings. The adjuster could be responsible for providing and entered chives are or injecting some humor during a break. This might enable people to take themselves less seriously while continuing to take their jobs and responsibilities seriously.

- Create a "1st aid kit". A kit that contains surefire stimuli that tickle your funny bone, include comedy tapes, jokes, riddles, cartoons etc.

- Humor can be a sign of the times, of the times you want to gain name recognition or your company, of the times you want to make your company seem inviting to potential customers. Here are some examples that others have used. On the plumber's truck: a flush beats a full house. On a magicians van: warning, a magician driving, may turn into a garage.

- Make a conscious effort to look and listen for relevant and funny work related things around you. Write them down immediately. Eventually you will build up a file of suitable material for speeches and presentations, which is the easiest and most logical way to use humor.

- Occasionally sprinkle internal correspondences with humor. As Joe Goodman, director of the humor project puts it, "humor sells ideas and improves the recall of those ideas, why do you think so many advertisements use it?"

- Practice predicting stressful situations you might encounter and prepare alternative humorous responses you might use. By practicing these responses, you will more likely be able to use humor to defuse the heat of the moment.

- Experiment with jokes. Take one, adapted to yourself and your work situation, and try it out with several coworkers.

- Smile more. This sounds simple, but some people, habitually do not smile. People who smile or better liked. Take yourself lightly and your work seriously. After all, work is very important.

- Be aware of people's sensitivities. As effective as humor can be, it is inappropriate when it makes you seem insensitive to an employee's basic concerns. For instance, regarding salary levels.

- And perhaps most important of all, focus humor on yourself and work situation, not on other people.

- Learn to look for something humorous and every situation; finding the funny side will help you keep a healthy perspective. Think funny and adopt an attitude of playfulness. This is not a license to be outrageous, but an openness to allow your mind to make room for the uncensored, the silly, and the childlike. Take your job and responsibilities seriously, but yourself lightly.

- Be able to take a joke: laughing at yourself and work situations will make it easier for others to do the same in the face of their problems.

- Keep a picture out with your favorite cartoons and a humor journal of laughable experiences. Look at them when you need some endorphins to lighten your load. Keep a DVD of your favorite comedy programs. Set up an office bulletin board for workers to share cartoons, funny signs, anecdotes, and sayings.

- Look for real-life anecdotes that you can use to make points and talking with others. A good story is worth 1000 pictures and is usually more relevant than jokes that tend to be forced.

- Cultivate humorous statements you can use in talking to yourself in order to break the urgency stress cycle: this, too, shall pass "it could be worse I could be ..."

- Take time to life and smile on-the-job. Serious people are seen as distant, negative, arrogant, or intimidating. Rather than fly the slaughter, use honey.

- Acknowledge your own humor style and stretch yourself to develop and integrate other styles.

- Buy books with humorous stories, quotes, or jokes, and find some that you can personalize.

- Offer a prize for a week to the employee who comes in with the most appropriate humor for whatever is happening at work that week. For instance, the busy president of one company received a "take a number" dispenser as a gift.

- Put something humorous in your own office that also makes the point. One boss had a life-size picture of her infant grandson with his foot in his mouth, and she captioned it, "don't let our customers catch you this way."

- Another manager had a "crisis meter" for his door. The chart heading movable arrow with such readings as "all clear", "batten down the hatches", "watch your step", and "meltdown". He changed the arrow as a situation developed. On one occasion, two staffers embroiled in an argument were reduced to laughter when he stood up and change the meter reading.

- When appropriate, allow for humor in some of your memos and correspondences. Thomas Edison interspersed humorous sayings in the margins of his ponderous experiment notebooks to lighten the load for his overworked assistants. History hasn't diminished his accomplishments for doing so. Allen Piece in his humor seminar mentioned having a joke as a P. S. without the punch line. People will keep the letter for a long time and will more often than not call to find out the answer to the joke.

- If you hire a professional writer for your speeches, hire one who knows how to write humor tailored to your personality and style.

- Take a humor awareness course at your local college or university and their continued education program. You will be exposed to other business people and will have the advantage of contrasting the atmosphere in your workplace with other businesses.

- Bring in a humor consultant who can do some on the job problem solving with you, your managers, and your employees, and who will make suggestions tailored for your business.

- Take a humor break yourself, at least once a day.

- Committing to find, decide that you're going to make your organization a more enjoyable place for people to be. Your commitment to this will be among your most important contributions.

- Create challenging work, some top executives will tell you that challenge is one of the most fun parts of their work. A leadership expert recently confirmed this finding. He said, "Where there are leaders, work is stimulating, challenging, fascinating, and fun."

- Reward and recognize: being rewarded and recognized is often part of people's experience of fun in their work. Often, all you need to do is pat someone on the back and say, "thanks" or "I really appreciate your work and value you as an employee". Beyond this, there are other things you might try to create an even greater sense of enthusiasm and excitement.

- Give out "super person of the month awards" for the best contribution to the company's zero defects goal.

- Consider holding contests. Contest can be unrelated to the work being done, but you can also use a contest quite effectively as a motivating tool for creativity, productivity, and customer service.

- Employ fun people, recall that people's personal intentions are vital to having fun at work. It may be that those intentions are more easily selected and trained. So, try to hire people who are capable of having fun, who are interested in having fun, and who believe in fun.

- Increase awareness in the organization of the issue of fun, through training, and through your own behavior. This may sound obvious, but it's deceptively complex. Because we need to ask, "Why do some people try to make work fun, and other people don't?" The answer: personal beliefs about the effects and importance of fun in work.

- Witty words: include humor in some of your letters, memorandums, minutes, and reports. Inject it in your major publications: catalogs, brochures, sales flyers, policy manuals, etc. Include a humor section in your company newsletter.

- Decorate: try brightening up your office or meeting rooms with humorous posters, pictures, etc.

- Phony policies: issue hilarious policies or procedures on official company letterhead. Send out a crazy directive on sick leave, vacation travel or any topic which is applicable or pending in your organization.

- Pins and buttons: decorate yourself by wearing pins were buttons with funny messages. For a meeting which promises to be stress filled, wear a button which reads, "Save time... See it my way!"

- Staff development: offer a program on humor to all staff. Stress the positive benefits of laughter brings to an organization. Work with a professional humor advisor and/or staff from other "humorized" companies.

- Speeches and presentations: give boost to your material as well as your audience by humorizing your talks. Use funny quotes, amusing anecdotes, self-deprecating humor, and quirky observations.

- Unusual events: schedule "stress buster" events on days when the going gets really tough. Encourage all staff to dress up on Halloween and sponsor a costume contest. I have worked for a company who all get dressed up and open late on Halloween. During the deepest despair of winter, try a cabin fever break out day to lift spirits. Consider having a couple of crazy hat and tie Fridays throughout the year. Plan something crazy for April Fools' Day, national left-handers Day (yes, there is one). Celebrate March as national humor month. Be creative!

- Celebrations: surprise your staff by having their office colorfully decorated when they arrived for work on their birthday. Consider really doing it up on "decade" birthdays.

- Humor group. Establish a humor group whose purpose is to plan and implement a variety of different activities for dates and events throughout the year. Humor is infectious. Have as many people as possible infect your organization with mirth!

- Send jokes via the Internet or in the mail to your friends. With jokes you send via e-mail, mark the envelope "personal" or "urgent".

- Every month I sent one person a special certificate saying thank you for helping me or for just being a good friend.

- I give out "permissible to be childlike" certificates to people I meet.

- I wear fun ties and fun clothing. I had a special red and black suit made for those important business occasions.

- Make up fun surveys for employees asking crazy questions like "when was the last time you had the urge to wiggle your ears?"

- Listen to what children have to say and learn to appreciate their humor. They have so much to offer. Make a list of the funny things you observe children doing or saying and let others read the list.

- If you have children, keep a humor log and give it to them when they are adults.

- There are examples of humor around us every day. Take notice of some of the funny signs in your area.

- Make up a collection of funny quotes and sayings. My collection consist of thousands of sayings, for example: "I feel good about this one"–Gen. George Armstrong Custer at Little Big Horn.

- My dentist uses humor to help me grin. His sign in his examination room says, "3 out of 5 dentists surveyed encourage daily flossing as a preventative measure for proper oral hygiene. The other two suggests that you "brush really, really hard".

- I love looking through old videos and photos with family and going back down memory lane. It always creates a lot of laughter.

- On the back of your door at work hang a notice or cartoon that you find funny, something like, "tell me again why I work here??" So that the 1st thing in the morning when you take your coat off you get a chance to smile and laugh.

- My grandfather and I often told jokes when doing chores. It sure lightened things up. Remember, "Time flies when you're having fun."

- If the office is feeling a little stressed, take a 1 min. "crazy" break and go into some song and dance. It will certainly clear the air and re-energize you.

- When frustrated with teenage-like employee demands, simply think yourself, "how could you take anyone who acts like this so seriously?"

- When I was a substitute teacher, I kept a notebook of some of the funny things students said, I would then share these with other teachers.

- Keep an eye out for unintentional humor in the newspaper advertisements.

- When I send out correspondences I always include an unfinished joke as a PS. This way the client , 9 out of 10 times, calls me to get the answer.

- I always have funny quotes in my wallet and checkbook, so I can laugh all the way to the bank. It also reminds me that I can laugh or I can cry when I see how little money is in there!

- At a staff meeting each week, have each member bring in a favorite cartoon of the week in a bag. When moving from one agenda to the next, pull out one of the cartoons, read it, and try to guess which person brought it.

- I belonged to a business organization who met every Thursday morning for breakfast. The first thing on the agenda was for everyone to get up and give a funny quote of the week. This always got memebers in the right mood for the meeting.

- Draw funny caricatures of yourself using other people's descriptions. Leave the caricatures for them to find–they will find you and you can share the laugh.

- I send postcards from my travels around the world to a friend who has a concrete gnome in his backyard. To this day he has no idea who is sending the gnome the postcards.

- Next time you are making lunch for someone, put a little joke or humorous note under the lunch.

- At times I am absent-minded. I make fun of this by asking very good friends, "Don't I know you from somewhere?".

- I collect stories of people who have played with stress successfully. I like the one from "laughing matters" magazine in which a waitress was being hassled by a customer who complained about everything. After serving him dinner, the customer quickly announced that his potato was bad. The waitress picked up the potato, slapped it a few times, saying "bad potato!" She then turned to the customer and told him to call her if the potato gave him anymore trouble. From that point on, he only gave her smiles.

- Put a sign on your office door, "why be normal?". People will always smile as they enter.

- Make up your own fortune cookies to share with others if you have guest over for dinner.

- I carry a picture of my kids and my wallet. It is a picture of 3 baby goats. I ask people if they would like to see my 3 kids.

- When I was in high school, I remember my teacher giving out lifesavers during test to lighten and sweeten what was for some a distasteful experience.

- Whenever I go away, I always like to look for toys, props, and humorous books to read and play with and bring back as presents for friends and family.

- A sign in the manager's office read, "You don't have to be crazy to work here...we will train you!"

- I have been to office parties where they still play "pin the tail on the donkey". It enables people to get in touch with their inner child and have fun.

- To develop my comic vision, I look for examples of humor and irony in the environment, then photographed them.

- Take photos of the office staff, place them on the bulletin board, input word bubbles with Post-it notes on the photos. Remember not to offend.

- Food can also be funding creates smiles. Quite often I'll give out lollipops, ice cream, and popcorn which bring out the child in us.

- Listen to comedy tapes while driving to work, you'll be amazed at how time flies when you're having fun.

- If you have to go to a meeting that is going to be on the dull side, tell them that you'll be there with bells on, when you turn up have little bells on your belt.

- Leave jokes and cartoons lying around for people to discover. A telephone booth is a great place.

- If you are at a tollbooth and pay to get over a bridge, pay for the person behind you and watch the reaction.

- Read 10–20 pages every day of a funny book.

- Include cartoons and funny stories with your newsletters.

- Bring in outside speakers for in-service programs on humor in the workplace.

- Leave funny messages on your voicemail such as "I don't want to bore you with metaphysics, but how do you know this is voicemail? Maybe it's a dream, or maybe it's an illusion, or maybe you don't really exist. One way to find out is to leave a message, and if it's reality, I will call you back".

- Learn to juggle, and then teach others at work.

- Learn a magic trick, and then teach others at work.

- Purchase a Rolodex and turn it into an instant humor resource. Write humorous or motivational sayings on each card and file them alphabetically by topic. Great to use while on hold on the phone.

- Recycle bubble wrap packing material. This is a great stress relief and an invitation for others to smile.

- Purchase a joke of the day and cartoon of the day calendar. Hand out the jokes and cartoons to people you come across.

- Send crazy gifts to friends.

- Put humorous pictures on your refrigerator door.

- Put your children's artwork on the refrigerator door. Encourage employees to hang them up at work.

- Incorporate humor in the e-mails you send. It will make the recipient take note of what you are trying to say.

- I love going out with my friends and talking about embarrassing moments. It's a way of sharing blasts from the past with blasts from the past.

- When driving with children in the car on a long journey, have them look out for funny signs.

- Create a list of good thoughts.

- Use reverse psychology for humor. I love the story of a person who was living in New York City during the garbage strike; they wrapped up their garbage like presence so that it would be stolen each night.

- Go and see live comedy shows.

- Record and video children at play. Presented to them later in life. It will be a legacy of laughter.

- Send incorrect birthday cards to friends and family, for example; send a 2-year-old card to your 69-year-old grandmother.

- Sponsor a staff development program on humor.

- Sponsor a costume contest at work with different themes.

- Make up a treasure hunt at work.

- Encourage a day where everyone wears T-shirts that are fun, with funny sayings, or cartoons.

- Visit the toy store at least once a month.

- Put up employee baby photos and have competitions were people have to match names to photos..

- Organize a paper airplane flying contest in the office.

- Write a laughter contract with yourself.

Appendix A:

Abra-KID-abra Activity Book

Years ago, I toured doing my motivational kid's show for elementary schools. I called it the "Kids First" show. I met thousands of kids and to this day, still have some that contact me on a regular basis. Following, is my kids activity book that I gave out to the children I was lucky enough to meet.

Adding these pages to this book, have brought back so many memories of interesting shows, laughing children, and the wonderful people that made me what I am today. I learned so much about being a real performer during those years. I learned how to deal with any unforseen circumstances and less than ideal performance situations. Most of all, I learned how to perform for every walk of life and age. How to keep the administrators and teachers laughing as much as the children, and how to make them want to have you back again.

I hope you share these with a young person you know and enjoy the sense of wonder I witnessed from those stages so many years ago.

Abra-KID-abra!
WELCOME!

Welcome to the wonderful world of magic, fun and excitement!

This is your **"Abra-KID-abra"** Magic, Coloring, And Activity Fun Book. In it you will find all sorts of exciting and fun tricks, activities and adventures to enjoy.

Magic is thousands of years old. Ancient secrets of some of the world's best magicians are told here. Enjoy having fun with your friends while showing them some of the amazing tricks you'll learn in the pages of this book. Remember part of the power and mystique of magic is in the **secrets**!

☐ The first rule of magic is **NEVER tell how the trick is done!**

☐ The second rule of magic is **never do the same trick twice for the same audience!**

☐ The third rule of magic, which really "should be" the very **first** rule of magic, is to **always practice your magic before you show it to anybody.** We have purposefully selected simple magic tricks that have high impact and are guaranteed to amaze your friends and family!

Please enjoy all there is to do and learn with your very own
"Abra-KID-abra!" *Magic, Coloring and Activity Fun Book!*

Magically,

261

A-MAZE-ING!

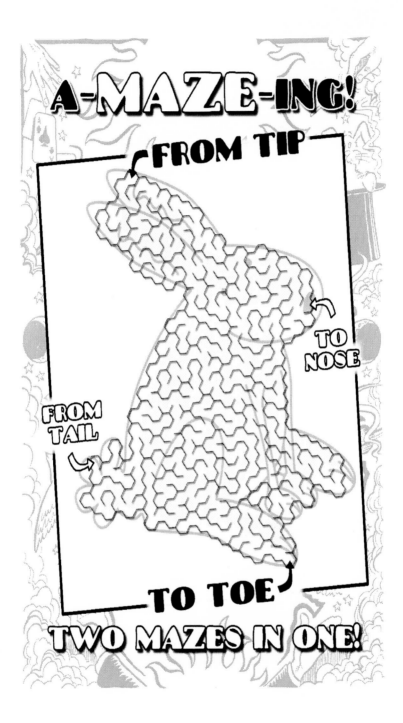

FROM TIP

TO NOSE

FROM TAIL

TO TOE

TWO MAZES IN ONE!

Christopher
interactive comedy

Funny Stuff:

What do Porcupines say to each other when they shake hands?
"Ouch!"

How do you know that carrots are good for your eyesight?
Have you ever seen a rabbit wearing glasses?

What kind of cat shouldn't you play cards with?
A Cheetah!

How do you make an elephant float?
Add an elephant to 2 scoops of vanilla ice cream & some milk!

What has no beginning, no end, and nothing in the middle?
A doughnut!

The MAGIC Rings!

MAGIC YOU CAN DO

COLOR SENSE

MARK THUMBNAIL WITH CRAYON

What the Audience Sees: You amazingly identify the color of a crayon handed to you behind your back only by touching it.

Super-Secret Tricky Method: Ask someone to take any crayon from a box and hand it to you behind your back. Make sure you don't see it! You then turn to face the audience but keep the crayon behind your back. Secretly dig your right thumb-nail into the crayon wax. Keep hold of the crayon behind your back as you bring your right hand up to your forehead as if concentrating. Take a quick peek at your thumbnail and you will see bits of crayon in it and will know the chosen color. Fake concentrating some more and then dramatically announce the color!

FROM NOT TO KNOT

Effect: A knot mysteriously appears in the corner of a handkerchief.

Secret: Before your performance, secretly tie a knot in one corner of a handkerchief. Show the handkerchief but hold it with the knot hidden in your right hand. The left hand now lifts the bottom end of the handkerchief and places it in the right hand along with the top corner. Give the handkerchief a shake and drop the unknotted end. Repeat this three times. On the third attempt allow the knotted corner to drop, retaining your grip on the other corner. All you have done is change the corner you are holding but it appears that the knot has formed by magic.

KNOT

THIRD TIME DROP KNOTTED END

267

JUMPING BAND

Put a rubber band around your first and second fingers so that it looks like figure 1 from the front. As you stretch the rubber band, secretly put all your fingertips inside the band. This is not seen by the audience.

Tell them the rubber band will amazingly jump across to the other two fingers. All you need to do is straighten out your fingers, and the band will move to the other fingers as in figure 3.

COOL MAGIC TRICKS

DO NOT EVER SHOW THIS SIDE OF YOUR HAND

ELboW Grease

Show everyone a single coin. Tell all that by rubbing your elbow with it, you can change it into two coins! And you do it!

Before doing this trick hide a similar coin in your collar (fig.1) as you rub your elbow, grasp the hidden coin and, as you bring your hands together, you can show your audience two coins where there was once just one!!!

HIDDEN COIN

RUB COIN ON ELBOW

FIG. 1.

Acrobatic Clips!

Fold a dollar bill in an 'S' shape, and attach two paperclips as shown below. Tell everybody that the paperclips will be launched into the air, and in the middle of thier acrobatic flight, will come together and impossibly link... right in mid-air!

With a drumroll, pull the two ends of the bill sharply in opposite directions. The clips will come together and jump into the air all by themselves. Now you just need to catch the paperclips, show them linked together, and take your bow!

OPTICAL ILLUSIONS

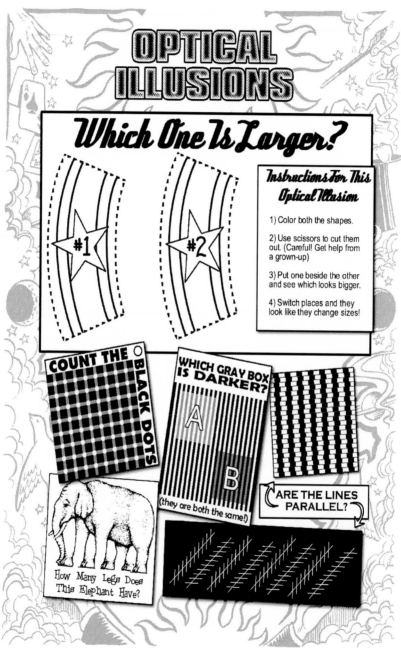

Which One Is Larger?

#1 #2

Instructions For This Optical Illusion

1) Color both the shapes.

2) Use scissors to cut them out. (Careful! Get help from a grown-up)

3) Put one beside the other and see which looks bigger.

4) Switch places and they look like they change sizes!

COUNT THE BLACK DOTS

WHICH GRAY BOX IS DARKER?

A

B

(they are both the same!)

ARE THE LINES PARALLEL?

How Many Legs Does This Elephant Have?

RUBBER PENCIL

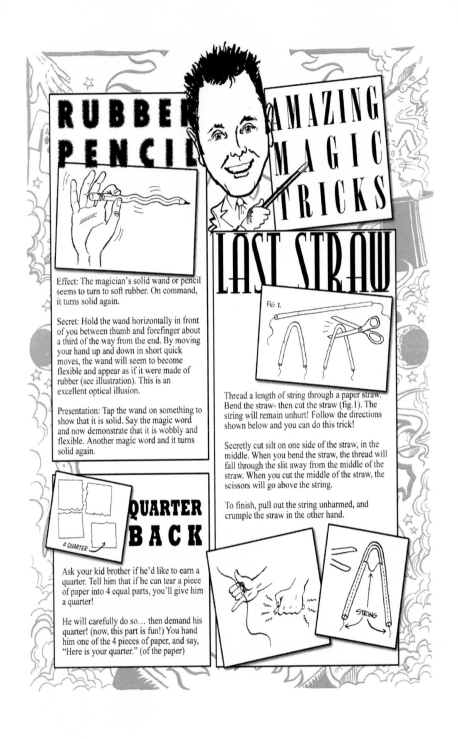

AMAZING MAGIC TRICKS

LAST STRAW

Effect: The magician's solid wand or pencil seems to turn to soft rubber. On command, it turns solid again.

Secret: Hold the wand horizontally in front of you between thumb and forefinger about a third of the way from the end. By moving your hand up and down in short quick moves, the wand will seem to become flexible and appear as if it were made of rubber (see illustration). This is an excellent optical illusion.

Presentation: Tap the wand on something to show that it is solid. Say the magic word and now demonstrate that it is wobbly and flexible. Another magic word and it turns solid again.

FIG 1.

Thread a length of string through a paper straw. Bend the straw- then cut the straw (fig.1). The string will remain unhurt! Follow the directions shown below and you can do this trick!

Secretly cut silt on one side of the straw, in the middle. When you bend the straw, the thread will fall through the slit away from the middle of the straw. When you cut the middle of the straw, the scissors will go above the string.

To finish, pull out the string unharmed, and crumple the straw in the other hand.

QUARTER BACK

A QUARTER

Ask your kid brother if he'd like to earn a quarter. Tell him that if he can tear a piece of paper into 4 equal parts, you'll give him a quarter!

He will carefully do so... then demand his quarter! (now, this part is fun!) You hand him one of the 4 pieces of paper, and say, "Here is your quarter." (of the paper)

STRING

AMAZING but oh so easy MAGIC

PENCiL POWER

Effect: The magician makes some mysterious passes around a wand or pencil which uncannily starts to move on its own.

Secret: The magician secretly blows on the wand, which causes it to roll.

Props: Use a wand or pencil, and a smooth table-top.

Preparation: Practice blowing toward the wand gently and secretly.

Presentation: Lay the wand on the table and very slowly trace circles around the outside of the wand with a finger. Then, as you move the finger away, the wand seems to follow. You claim to have created a static field that pulls plastic like a magnet. The trick is that as you draw the finger away from you and from the wand, you blow gently on the wand. The audience is so busy watching the movement of the finger, they won't notice that you are blowing towards the wand, which causes it to roll easily on the flat surface.

VANISHING RUBBER BANDS

Wrap a rubber band around the tips of both your middle fingers (fig.1). On the edge of a table, show these two fingers (fig.2).

FIG. 1.

FIG. 2.

Place both hands under the table edge (fig.3). Then show both index fingers and say, "The rubber bands have disappeared!" (fig.4)

Place both hands under the table again, then show both middle fingers. With a surprised look on your face, declare, "The rubber bands have reappeared!"

FIG. 3.

FIG 4

Tricks

HYPNO-PENCIL

Tell your friends that you can hypnotize an ordinary lead pencil and make it write any color they ask you to!

"Make it write red!" says one. So with a flourish, do just that!

Any other color is just as easy to do!

X-RAY VISION

Ask someone to thoroughly shuffle a deck of cards. The cards are handed to you and you put them into the box they came in. You now remove the cards, one by one, but name each card before removing them!

You have, beforehand cut out a little window in the box. This allows you to see the name of the card you are about to show!

RING THING

Tell your pals that you can do an impossible trick!

You say that you can push your whole hand through a finger ring you are holding in your hand!

Of course none of them will believe you! With a big smile, put your finger through the ring and poke your hand. You are 'pushing' your hand through the ring!

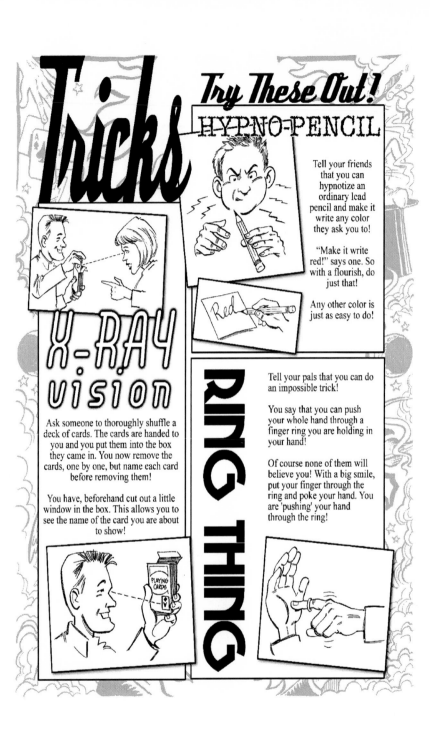

CONTACT INFORMATION:

Share your own personal stories and jokes with Christopher at funnyhypermagicboy.com or by emailing christopherjamescomedy@gmail.com.

Join the Facebook Fan Club: Search for Funny Hyper Magic Boy or go to www.facebook.com/funnyhypermagicboy.

Over 120 Youtube videos online. Visit funnyhypermagicboy.com for the latest links and updates.